THE CELTS

THE CELTS

LIFE, MYTH, AND ART

JULIETTE WOOD

Thorsons
Directions for Life

The Celts

Thorsons
An imprint of HarperCollins*Publishers*
77–85 Fulham Palace Road
Hammersmith, London, England W6 8JB

Published in the United States by Thorsons in 2002

Conceived, created and designed by Duncan Baird Publishers.

First published in Great Britain in 1998 by
Duncan Baird Publishers Ltd

Library of Congress Cataloging-in-Publication Data is available.

1 3 5 7 9 10 8 6 4 2

ISBN: 0-00-764059-5

Typeset in Perpetua and Bernhard Modern
Color reproduction by Colourscan, Singapore
Printed and bound in Singapore by Imago

NOTE
The abbreviations CE and BCE are used throughout this book:
CE Common Era (the equivalent of AD)
BCE Before the Common Era (the equivalent of BC)

HALF–TITLE PAGE **Iron spearhead with decorative bronze applications found in the Thames river, London (3rd–2nd centuries BCE).**

FRONTISPIECE **The Burren, Co. Clare, Ireland.**

TITLE PAGE **Bronze male head-mask found in Montsérié, Hautes Pyrenees, France (ca. 2nd century CE).**

CONTENTS

IMAGE AND
IMAGINATION 6

The Soul of the Celts 8

The Story of the Celts 10

*Map: the Ancient Celtic
World 11*

The Wealth of Kings 14

Castell Henllys, Wales 16

The Art of the Celts 18

Sacred Spirals 22

Unlocking the Mysteries 24

VISIONS OF THE
NATURAL WORLD 26

Images of Divinity 28

Spirits of Place 32

The Waters of Life 34

Snowdonia, Wales 38

The Fish of Wisdom 40

The Divine Female 42

The "Paps of Anu," Ireland 46

Mythic Creatures 48

The Spirit of the Forest 50

The Tree of Life 54

The Black Forest,
Germany 56

Fantasies of Leaf
and Flower 58

Divine Trinities 60

On Wings of Divinity 64

Journeys to the
Otherworld 66

Poulnabrone, Ireland 70

THE LIVING BOOK 72

Design and Divinity 74

The Eternal Knot 78

The Glory of Kells 80

The Spirit of the Letter 82

Mortals, Saints, and Angels 84

The Image of Christ 88

Heavenly Creatures 90

IMAGE, BELIEF, AND
RITUAL 92

Magic and Metamorphosis 94

A Year of Festivals 98

Grianan Aileach, Ireland 100

Sacrifice and Ceremony 102

Keepers of Wisdom 104

Portents and Prophecies 108

Adornments and Amulets 110

Treasures of the Lord 114

The Cross of Life 118

THE IMMORTAL
HERO 120

A People at War 122

Dun Aengus, Ireland 126

The Face of the Warrior 128

Arms and Armor 130

Divine Steeds 134

**Pronunciation Guide and
Glossary 136**

Further Reading 137

Index 139

Picture Credits 144

IMAGE AND IMAGINATION

LEFT Lake Hallstatt, near Salzburg in Austria. Modern Europe first awoke to the complexity of ancient Celtic society in the mid-19th century, when Austrian archaeologists discovered the rich graves of Celts who had once lived on the lakeshore. From the 7th–5th centuries BCE the local salt deposits provided the Hallstatt Celts with the basis for prosperous trade.

Thousands of years ago, the Celts emerged in central Europe as a distinctive group of peoples with their own language, mythology, and art. From their heartlands, they migrated in all directions, fighting and trading with the alternative cultures they encountered, and leaving in their wake superbly crafted weaponry, jewelry, and household objects. Today, these spectacular artifacts allow us not only to follow the movements of the Celts over land, but also to appreciate the artistic brilliance and sophisticated vision of a civilization that, at its height, stretched from Ireland to Turkey.

BELOW This bronze head, dating from ca. 400–350BCE and found at Dürrnberg in Austria, once decorated a wooden flagon. The prominent eyes and perfect symmetry of the moustache, eyebrows, hair, and mouth are typical of the simple style used to depict faces in the early period of Celtic art.

THE SOUL OF THE CELTS

An armed figure and two dogs attacking a bull decorate this silver-gilt panel, which forms the base of a cauldron found at Gundestrup in Denmark but of Celtic manufacture. Such figures evoke the supernatural hunts described in the later Celtic hero tales of, for example, Ireland and Wales.

More than two thousand years ago, Europe north of the Mediterranean was dominated by the Celts, a collection of peoples with shared traditions of language, art, and culture. Most of what we know about ancient Celtic customs and society comes from contemporary writers in the Classical Mediterranean, for whom the people they called *Galatae*, *Keltoi*, or *Celtae* were fearsome but fascinating barbarians. Foreign observers were awestruck by the reckless bravery of the Celtic warrior and what they saw as a general fondness for warfare. Even off the battlefield, the Celts clearly possessed an ebullience that left a mark on visitors from the more restrained Classical world. "Quarrelsome," "proud," "frank," "insolent," "boastful," and "high-spirited" are among the Greek and Roman descriptions of the Celtic character.

Much of what the Classical writers say about Celtic lifestyle resonates with what we know from the later, native Celtic sources of, for example, Ireland. The verbal arts were prized as greatly as all the skills of war, but Classical writers rarely mention the incredible inheritance of information through oral art, nor the logic or beauty of Celtic manuscript. Of course, they had no knowledge of Celtic language, so bardic skills were altogether lost on them and manuscripts indecipherable. For the Greeks and Romans, all Celts were

intriguing but essentially uncivilized and barbaric—a unified people held together by the common cause of war. But, as with most prejudiced outsiders, the Greeks and Romans generalized, creating a simplistic picture of the Celtic world, which at last modern archaeology has undone. We know now that the Celts formed a complex and varied group of societies rather than a homogeneous whole: social and religious customs differed widely between the Celtic lands, which by ca. 350BCE stretched from the Atlantic as far east as Turkey. Some Celtic peoples belonged to large and loose confederations, others to small, tightly-knit tribal units.

But undermining Classical theories does not stop there—the Celts were no more unsophisticated than they were a single set of people who were war mad. They were highly skilled miners, smiths, builders, farmers, and merchants with wide international connections. Celtic religion expressed beliefs about omens, magic, and transformation through the symbolism of the natural world. Classical artists preferred symmetry and order, but the Celts drew inspiration from the infinitely subtle mutability of nature. In the La Tène style of Celtic art—which began ca. 500BCE and found its last reverberations in the magnificent metalwork and manuscripts of early medieval Ireland—the merest suggestion of human, animal, or plant form might be achieved through the breathtaking command of curving, swirling lines of marvelous ingenuity and delicacy. While there is much about the Celts of which we remain ignorant, the surviving masterworks of Celtic art are an uncontestable witness to the glories of a truly great civilization.

This Romano-Celtic bronze statue from Bouray, France (2nd century BCE), shows a god with a torc around his neck and hooves on the ends of his crossed legs. These attributes suggest that he is probably a Celtic nature deity—the natural world was central to Celtic religion.

THE STORY OF THE CELTS

The earliest cultures that we term Celtic appeared in central Europe ca. 800BCE, beginning the first Celtic phase, known as the Hallstatt period, after an Austrian town near which many spectacular Celtic artifacts have been recovered. The Celtic world at this time stretched from the Balkans and Bohemia to what is now southern Germany. Between ca. 800BCE and ca. 300BCE, Celtic power expanded to include parts of central Turkey, Italy, Spain, Portugal, and France, and eventually Britain and Ireland. While the influence of the Celts on European prehistory was undoubtedly immense, no single set of cultural characteristics, much less psychological or spiritual ones, can adequately sum up what is meant by "Celtic" civilization. Celtic societies developed in response to a wide range of historical and geographical circumstances. In some areas, the Celts depended primarily on trade, but in others, the main activity was farming or stock breeding. Likewise, some groups were dominated by warrior élites or princely aristocracies, while others formed hybrid cultures with local ethnic groups.

The rich graves discovered at Hallstatt in the mid-nineteenth century and minutely recorded by the pioneer archaeologist Engels revealed both native and imported goods. Engels' work introduced the world to a sophisticated Iron Age society governed by a princely ruling class whose power lay in the control of nearby salt mines. They built impressive fortifications and were interred in burial mounds, often laid out on funerary carts amid much of their wealth. The later Hallstatt chiefdoms thrived on the international salt

Decorative neck-rings, known as torcs, were symbols of high status and divinity among the Celts. This gold torc with its ornate terminals was made in northern Spain during the 2nd to 1st centuries BCE.

THE ANCIENT CELTIC WORLD

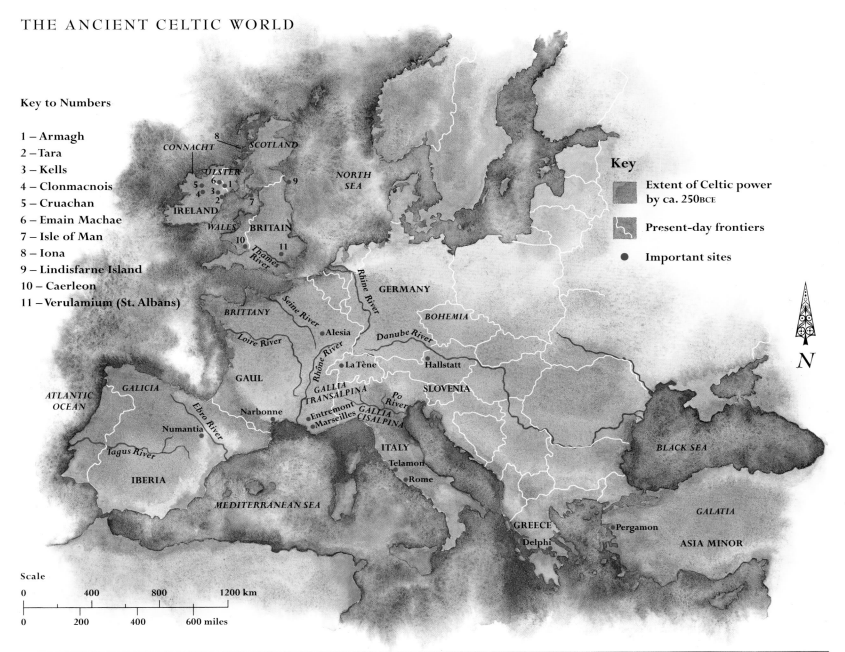

Key to Numbers

1 – Armagh
2 – Tara
3 – Kells
4 – Clonmacnois
5 – Cruachan
6 – Emain Machae
7 – Isle of Man
8 – Iona
9 – Lindisfarne Island
10 – Caerleon
11 – Verulamium (St. Albans)

Key

Extent of Celtic power
by ca. 250BCE

Present-day frontiers

● Important sites

Scale

0   400   800   1200 km

0   200   400   600 miles

Scenes of martial exercise adorn this bronze belt clasp (5th–6th centuries BCE) from the Slovenian Alps. A rider walks his horse, while athletes with "dumbells" spar at either side of a plumed warrior's helmet. At far right, a bird—a symbol of war—is perched on a pole or stylized tree.

trade, exploiting export routes down the Rhône river to the Greek colony of Marseilles, and beyond to the Classical Mediterranean.

Around the fifth century BCE, the focus of Celtic power shifted to a region from which the Celts could better exploit the Alpine trade routes to the increasingly powerful Etruscan centers of Italy. This period was characterized by a new style of art named after the Swiss site of La Tène, where artifacts decorated in the new way were first discovered. During the La Tène phase, Celtic civilization reached its far-thest extent: beautiful La Tène artwork has been recovered in every area of Celtic influence from the British Isles and the Iberian Peninsula to Asia Minor.

Soon, however, Celtic peoples came into direct conflict with the expanding Classical world. In 390BCE, Rome was sacked by Celts whom the Romans called *Galli* or "Gauls." Meanwhile, other Celtic groups moved through the Balkans and into Greece, and are thought to have attacked the great Greek sanctuary of Delphi in 279BCE. The Greeks called these invaders *Keltoi* or *Galatae*, whence the name Galatia in northern-central Turkey (see map, p.11). So appalled were the Greeks at the warring nature of the Celts, that one poet likened them to the mythical Titans, a race of fierce divine giants who fought against the Olympian gods. Nevertheless, the encounter of the Celtic and Classical worlds was marked by cultural absorption as much as by conflict, each learning from, as well as fighting with, the other.

By a turn of fate, during the third century BCE, the autonomous Celtic tribes found themselves sandwiched between two expanding cultures: the Romans to the south and the Germanic tribes to the north. In the many battles between the Romans and the Celts, two particularly stand out as marking the end of Celtic power on the European mainland: the Roman victories at Telamon in Italy in 225BCE, and at Alesia in Gaul in 52BCE. From this time onward, the Celtic culture of continental Europe was in retreat, and by ca. 500CE, it had virtually disappeared altogether. However, in Ireland, the far western outpost of Celtic power, this ancient culture was to enjoy one last, magnificent golden age.

This exquisite gold brooch from Spain (ca. 3rd century BCE) combines Classical workmanship with Celtic themes. An Iberian warrior fights naked except for a large La Tène-style shield and a sword belt. Bracing himself against the arch of the brooch, the fighter bravely confronts an attacking lion.

THE WEALTH OF KINGS

Objects associated with ritual drinking were deposited in many early graves, especially during the Hallstatt and La Tène periods. The delicate gold openwork of this design from a 5th-century-BCE grave near Schwarzenbach in the Rhineland, Germany, once fitted a wooden bowl.

Archaeological discoveries of aristocratic adornments present the Celts as a people who made no secret of their wealth. Princely tombs filled with magnificent jewelry and lavishly decorated ceremonial artifacts abound in all corners of the Celtic world, but especially in the central Rhineland and Switzerland. Gold and silver-gilt pieces, ranging from cauldrons and cup-trimmings to brooches, bracelets, and torcs, display all the principles of stylized, spiral, and curvilinear decoration, as well as patterns and forms taken from nature—leaf shapes, flower designs, and birds and beasts snake across every shiny surface. It is believed that Celtic chieftains had engravers in their service who would produce pieces of ornamented metalware to their precise specifications.

Gold and silver did have a practical use too, however, when the increase in Celtic trade meant that barter was no longer an effective method of exchange. Taking a lead from the Greeks and Romans, the Celts began to mint their own coins. Initially based on Classical designs, they soon displayed the unmistakable motifs of Celtic decorative style. For example, the horses and chariot of Apollo, an image used on the reverse of some Greek coins, gave way to Celtic horse imagery. The obverse ("heads") sides of Celtic coins largely show warrior-aristocratic faces with stiff, lime-washed hairstyles, although some do seem to imitate Roman styles: coins minted in Britain ca. 10BCE by the Celtic king Cunobelinos, ruler of the Catuvellauni tribe, romanize the leader's features and bear a latinized form of his name.

ABOVE Celtic tribes began to mint coins in imitation of Mediterranean styles. This hoard contains some Roman silver coins, but Celtic artists adapted Classical symbolism for their own use.

RIGHT This spectacular brooch, known as the "Tara Brooch," is one of the most famous examples of early 8th-century Irish metalwork. Found in a box on the beach at Bettystown, Co. Meath, the enamel and millefiori glass insets add brilliant color to the silver-gilt and copper filigree.

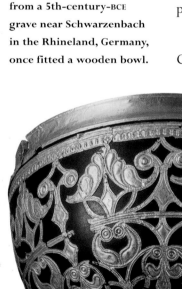

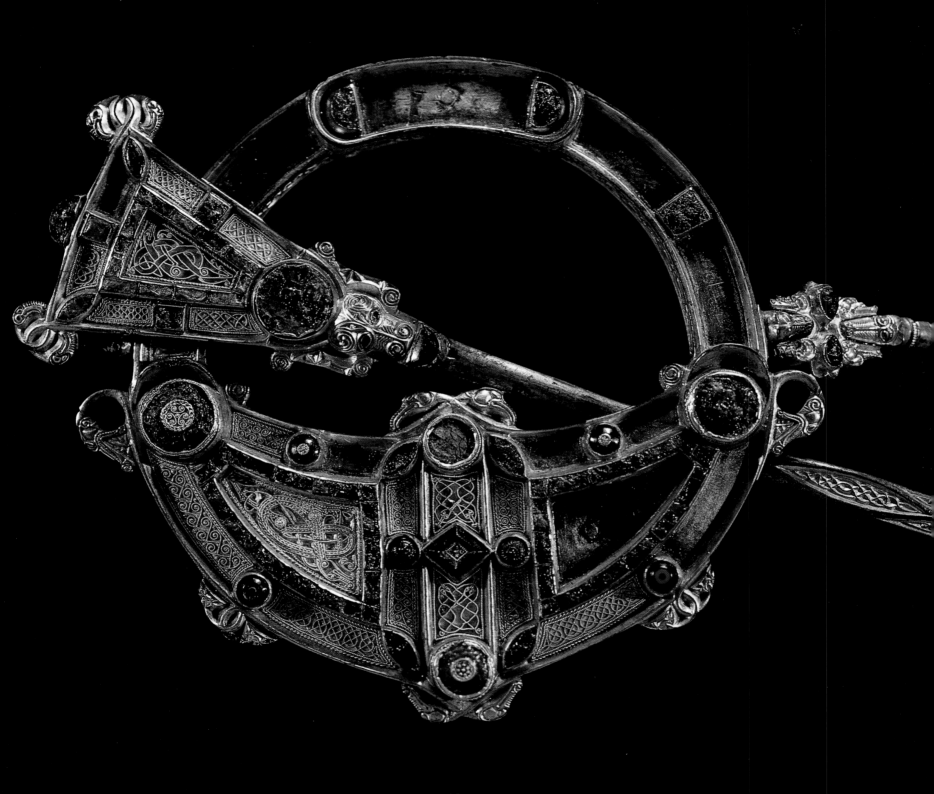

CASTELL HENLLYS, WALES
These round houses, which
have been reconstructed on
their original site at Castell
Henllys near Newport,
Pembrokeshire, would have
been typical dwellings for
the Iron Age Celts. Lengths
of timber radiating from a
central pole formed a
conical framework that was
attached to a ring of
vertical posts secured in
the ground. The structure
was then thatched and an
aperture was made in the
roof to allow smoke to
escape from a centrally
placed hearth. The low
walls were constructed of
wattle and daub. Villages
of roundhouses existed
mainly in lowland areas of
Britain, where fuel and the
wood and reeds necessary
for construction were
plentiful.

THE ART OF THE CELTS

The Celtic pottery and metalwork of the Hallstatt period (ca. 800BCE–ca. 500BCE) were decorated with strikingly simple geometric designs. Artisans copied prestigious foreign imports, such as jars from Attica in Greece, and adapted the motifs to suit indigenous tastes. However, the most enduring legacy of Celtic art is the beautiful curvilinear form of decoration known as the La Tène style. The interlaced La Tène patterns that adorn early Celtic metalwork survived across centuries of Celtic art, and eventually inspired the spectacular decoration on early medieval Irish manuscripts. We might be surprised to learn, therefore, that these typical Celtic patterns actually represent an enormously cosmopolitan array of sources. For example, swirling Celtic motifs have both Classical and Near Eastern precedents. The great achievement of Celtic art lies less in the individual elements of its style than in its original synthesis of those elements, which continued to create a distinct aesthetic that then developed, under its own impetus and momentum, into the many strands of the later La Tène.

The art of the La Tène style, in its early forms, varied from intricate geometric designs, skillfully laid out with compasses, to highly stylized plant and animal motifs. However, by the middle of the fifth century BCE, a characteristic curvilinear style had emerged, which spread via trade and other contacts throughout the rapidly expanding Celtic world. Incised or raised patterns, exhibiting a characteristic tension between symmetry and asymmetry, began to appear on the surfaces of bronze or gold brooches and torcs (neck-rings). Coral and glass inlays added bright color and rich texture to both jewelry and weapons. British smiths crafted mirrors decorated with engraved designs of asymmetrical, but finely balanced, patterns in which the faces of bird-like creatures seem to appear and retreat. After smiths in

A miniature horse and rider surmount this 7th-century-BCE bronze axe-head found near Hallstatt in Austria. The simple style of both horse and man are characteristic of Celtic art of the period.

RIGHT Decorative bronze disks were a feature of chariots and horse harnesses. This one, from the grave of a 5th- or 4th-century-BCE warrior, is approximately 4 inches (11cm) in diameter with openwork bosses and adorned with an intricate pattern that would have been laid out using compasses.

A sculpture from the entrance to the sanctuary of the Saluvii, a
southern Gaulish tribe, at Roquepertuse, France. It shows two heads
held in the beak of a bird of prey. The two heads are influenced by
Hellenistic art and at one time would have been painted.

Britain and Ireland had mastered the technique of enameling, they created even more spectacular patterns, seen on ring brooches, shields, and scabbards (see illustration, p.15).

Despite the unquestionable beauty and technical brilliance of Celtic art, the precise meanings of its symbols are often difficult to establish. Classical sources note the Celts' love of metaphor and conundrum, and perhaps the intricate asymmetrical and abstract patterns of their art represent a visual version of the type of complex verbal patterns that characterize the later medieval literature of Ireland, Wales, and Brittany.

One possible reason for the lavish adornment found in Celtic art is a close relationship between art and patronage. The elaborate decoration on such a variety of prestigious objects suggests a powerful aristocracy making a dramatic show of its status. Further testimony to this assumption lies in the portability of much La Tène art: small but magnificently crafted pieces of jewelry, flamboyant cloths, and intricately decorated weapons were easy for aristocratic patrons to carry around as traveling symbols of their wealth.

Celtic art is also famous for its fine stone carving, a comparatively late innovation. Stone figurines became widespread during the Romano-Celtic period under the influence of Classical culture, while the arrival of Christianity saw the erection of intricately sculpted stone crosses (see pp.118–9) and other monuments.

La Tène design provided inspiration for the Irish style of manuscript decoration. Irish artists created patterns of such splendor, complexity, and delicacy that one observer called them the "work of angels" —the final flowering of a glorious imaginative heritage.

This piece of horse harness (1st century BCE, found in London, England) combines practical use with exquisite workmanship. The fine openwork design and vibrantly colored enamel are typical of the decorative horse tackle recovered from votive deposits and hoards all over Celtic Europe. Such attention to detail highlights the economic and religious importance of the horse in Celtic culture.

SACRED SPIRALS

The swirling, spiraling patterns of La Tène art decorate creations in a
vast range of media, from small, gold sacred objects to massive stone
monuments. These curvilinear designs suggest that Celtic artists
abhorred a vacuum, filling every space. In producing what, to many,
is the most characteristically "Celtic" art, they abandoned strict
symmetry for fluid patterns, in which the shapes of humans and
beasts emerge and dissolve before our eyes. Palmette and lotus
motifs, borrowed from the Classical world, display the cosmopolitan
nature of Celtic art, while stunning circular forms display its power.

UNLOCKING THE MYSTERIES

The ancient Celts have long been associated with mystery—as if the creators of Celtic art and literature had used a secret code that keeps us guessing as to the meaning of their work. These gifted peoples have excited the imagination of countless observers, but our knowledge of them comes mainly from archaeological findings and Classical written sources. The only written testimony left by the Celts themselves is found in a few inscriptions in Greek or Latin and medieval literature.

Classical sources claim that the ancient Celts had no written language, but the discovery of such inscriptions has undermined these claims and the implication that the Celts were a primitive people. Certainly, the sophistication of ancient Celtic art presupposes a complex society, which in turn implies the existence of a developed legal and political system.

In the area of Roman influence, Latin was used to spell out Celtic names, especially on coins. Sometimes Celtic languages, such as Gaulish, were rendered in the Greek or Latin alphabet, most notably a bronze tablet of a legal text from Botoritta in Spain; a stone inscription from Gaul (see illustration, opposite); and the "Coligny Calendar," a bronze plaque listing the days, months, and festivals of the Celtic year in Gaulish (see p.99). Later, between the fifth and seventh centuries CE, a unique Irish script called Ogham was used to inscribe names and places on stone funerary monuments in Ireland and areas of Britain influenced by Irish

The silver-gilt Gundestrup Cauldron, thought to have been made in the Balkans ca. 1st century BCE, is a pictorial record of Celtic culture, around 1,000 years older than any surviving written account. As shown here, the inside right panel depicts a horned god (a god of nature) surrounded by animals; to his left is a procession of armed men; while the front panels show deity heads.

colonists. The script consists of clusters of strokes along a central line, and its appearance was probably inspired by the Roman numerical system. Most importantly, however, it was easy to carve on stone.

For the most part, though, information and myth were transmitted orally by trained professionals, who used elaborate mnemonic devices to conserve a complex intellectual heritage (see pp.104–7). Lists cataloging tales, laws, and proverbs, usually grouped in threes, and poetry in Irish and Welsh, suggest that the ancient oral transmission continued into medieval times for long enough to be written down.

The inscription on this stone slab from Vaucluse, France (2nd–1st centuries BCE), is in Gaulish using Greek letters. The top line in this photograph shows a man's name, Segomaros. The remaining text is part of a dedication from him to a local goddess called Belesama.

VISIONS OF THE NATURAL WORLD

Nature, with its endless permutations of mountains, rivers, lakes, forests, trees, and animals, its boundless earth and neverending sky, was sanctified by the Celts and, as a result, often became the focus of important Celtic ritual. The Greeks and Romans, who built elaborate temples, marveled that Celtic deities were worshipped at simple open-air shrines or in plain forest clearings. But the Celts' artistic response to the natural world was vigorous and imaginative. Nature provided a symbolic archive: animal and plant forms merge into spectacular patterns on jewelry, weapons, and household objects, to culminate in the vibrant decoration of medieval manuscripts.

LEFT The loch and Black Mountain on Rannoch Moor in the Scottish Highlands. Lakes were often the backdrops for shrines and rituals. Deities, usually female, presided over the sacred waters.

ABOVE AND LEFT These animal heads are the terminals of a heavy torc made of silver-gilt over an iron core (6th century BCE). It may have adorned a statue, probably of a nature deity. The creatures wear torcs.

IMAGES OF DIVINITY

This wheeled "chariot," found at Strettweg in Austria, depicts a female figure, perhaps a goddess, holding aloft a sacred cauldron. The woman is surrounded by stags and mounted huntsmen. The chariot is made of bronze and was found among the grave goods of a Hallstatt warrior of the 7th century BCE.

When the Galatians attacked the Greek sanctuary at Delphi in 279BCE, their leader Brennus is said to have laughed at the images of the Greek gods in human form—the Celts worshipped the forces of nature and did not initially envisage deities in anthropomorphic terms. Later, as the Roman empire expanded, Classical influence on Celtic art became unmistakable, and images of gods and goddesses in human form grew more common.

It is unlikely that a trans-Celtic religion ever existed, although a range of sun gods, sky gods, and mother goddesses do appear to have been venerated in all parts of the Celtic world. Sun gods are often identified by the attributes of wheels (a symbol of the sun), while sky gods are given hammers (symbolizing thunder) and thunderbolts. Mother goddesses (see pp.42–5) are recognizable from the domestic objects that are often seen accompanying them, such as loaves or linen.

Other divinities of wide importance included one that the Roman general Julius Caesar called "Mercury"—giving the deity the name of the Roman god whom the general thought most similar. According to Caesar, this divinity was paramount among the Gauls and was revered as the inventor of the arts and as a patron of commerce. However, the Celtic Mercury was apparently also connected with less peaceful activity, because he was sometimes called by the Gaulish epithets Artaios (which means "bear") and Moccus (which means "pig")—bears and pigs were considered to be sacred animals and were associated with war and hunting. In Gallo-Roman art, the god is often depicted in a similar aspect to the Classical Mercury, although he also appears with three faces, representing the importance of triplication in sacred Celtic iconography (see pp.60–63).

RIGHT A detail of a head from a cauldron of the 1st century BCE, found in a bog near Rynkeby in Denmark, but made farther south in the Celtic lands. The head was an important artistic and religious motif for the Celts. This figure, with a high-status torc and stylized hair, is likely to be a deity, perhaps a goddess.

LEFT **The name of this Romano-Celtic god, Taranis, means "thunderer." He is often shown holding a thunderbolt, which here he carries in his raised right hand. He is equivalent to the Classical god Jupiter.**

The actual name of the Celtic Mercury is unknown, but he is often associated with the Celtic god Lugos. It is difficult to identify images on any surviving artifacts with Lugos himself, but modern cities such as Lyons in France and Leiden in Holland recall the ancient place-name Lugdunum ("fortress of the god Lugus"). In the Irish tales, Lugh Samhildénach ("Lugh who possesses all the arts") is an important figure believed to be related to Lugos. But, most strikingly, two similar festivals existed relating to Lugos. They were held around the same time of year in both Lyons and Ireland: the August festival of Lugos in Lyons, and the traditional harvest festival of Lughnasa in Ireland on August 1. However, trans-Celtic deities such as Lugos tend to be the exception. More often, veneration was expressed locally, and about two-thirds of the divine names recorded in ancient inscriptions appear only once.

As Mercury-Lugos exemplifies, Celtic deities were believed to perform a variety of functions. Similarly, the Gallo-Roman god known as "Mars-Lenus," an important god of the Treveri tribe in north-eastern Gaul, was depicted as a warrior, but worshipped as a powerful healer god. Devotees at the Romano-Celtic sanctuary in Trier, the capital of the Treveri, called upon Mars-Lenus to protect children.

RIGHT **This head, the most sacred part of the body for the Celts, is nestled in carved foliage and decorates the handle of a 4th-century-BCE wine jug made of bronze. The flagon was recovered from a princely grave at Dürrnberg in Austria.**

Celtic images in metal and stone imply that cults devoted to divine couples were also popular. The goddess in the couple is always a purely Celtic deity, but sometimes the god is Roman or Romano-Celtic. For example, the Celtic goddess Rosmerta is often depicted as the consort of "Mercury." Rosmerta, whose name means "Great Provider," is most commonly represented with symbols of abundance and plenty, such as buckets of wine or honey, while "Mercury" is depicted with a hammer, perhaps in this case implying protection.

SPIRITS OF PLACE

This gorgon's head once adorned the main temple pediment at the sacred springs of Bath, England. It perfectly fuses Classical and Celtic belief: although identified as the Gorgon Medusa (a female sorceress from Classical myth), the carving's masculine appearance is distinctively Celtic in its aggressive stare, thick beard, and swirling hair.

Unless they lived in an area of strong Classical influence, the Celts rarely enclosed their places of worship in temples of stone, preferring to use nature's own boundaries, such as trees or the banks of a lake, to divorce sacred space from the secular world. Divinity was perceived to reside in all corners of the natural world—particularly around springs, groves, and lakes. If specially-constructed sanctuaries existed at all, they were either open to the sky, such as the wooden platforms near the lake's edge at La Tène, Switzerland, or built of wood and thatch, such as the central structure of Navan Fort in County Armagh, Ireland.

Forest groves were especially hallowed as natural spaces where people could gather to venerate gods and spirits. The word for "sacred grove" was *nemeton*, and it occurs widely throughout the Celtic world. The Greek writer Strabo (ca. 64BCE–ca. 21CE) claimed that the Celts of Galatia met annually at the "Drunemeton" ("Oak Sanctuary") to decide important religious and political issues. Similarly, the word forms part of Arnemetia, the local goddess of a British tribe of what is now Derbyshire, England, and its occurrence in the name of the Romano-Celtic god Mars Rigonemetis affords him the title "King of the Sacred Grove."

Features of a sacred landscape were often named for the local deity with whom they were associated. For example, the Ardennes forest on the border of France, Belgium, and Germany takes its name from the goddess Arduinna.

Rituals, too, reflected a concern with the sanctity of the natural world. Small offerings, believed to be to the soil to ensure the earth's fertility, were placed in domestic storage pits, while more elaborate deposits were left in specially dug ritual shafts.

Lough Conn in Co. Mayo, Ireland. In Celtic tales, lakes were often home to
shape-shifting supernatural beings. The Welsh poet-hero Taliesin began his
adventures in the dwelling of the witch Ceridwen, who lived beneath a lake.
In order to escape, Taliesin had to transform himself into a salmon.

THE WATERS OF LIFE

The association between water and spiritual power is evident in Europe as early as the Bronze Age, and veneration for water became a hallmark of Celtic religion. Rivers are prominent in Celtic myth, and many have a tutelary goddess, such as Matrona, deity of the French Marne. In Irish tradition, the name of the goddess Bóinn was given to the Boyne river after the deity was drowned there for interfering with a sacred well.

For the ancient Celts, there was no clear distinction between the practice of medicine and healing by supernatural means. A great deal of trust was placed in the curative powers of springs, which often became the sites of great sanctuaries. The deity Sequana, for example, who is often depicted standing in a duck-shaped boat, was the eponymous goddess of the Seine river in France, and her sacred healing-place lay among the springs at the headwaters of the river, in Burgundy.

During the Romano-Celtic period, a number of sanctuaries dedicated to other healer-deities were so popular that extensive baths and hostels for pilgrims were constructed at these sites. Among the best known is the sanctuary of the goddess Sulis Minerva at the ancient springs of Bath, England. The goddess's powers were believed to extend beyond healing to dispensing justice and delivering retribution on behalf of those who worshipped her. Devotees hoping for cures from the god Belenus, the Celtic equivalent of Apollo, the Roman god of medicine, offered figurines of infants and horses at his healing shrine at Sainte-Sabine in Burgundy.

Offerings such as weapons were thrown into sacred lakes or wells in order to attract the favor of the gods. This gilded scabbard and short sword, the hilt of which terminates in a distinctive antenna-like decoration, date from the Hallstatt period. Such highly decorative objects were probably symbols of rank rather than actual fighting weapons.

These bathing nymphs come from a Roman fort at High Rochester in Northumberland, England, and probably depict a local Celtic goddess in triplicate form who possessed three aspects. In Celtic myth, only goddesses—never male deities—were associated with freshwater.

Larger bodies of water, such as lakes, were important sites for ritual activity. The Greek author Strabo mentions a sacred lake near Toulouse in France, said to be filled with treasure that no one dared steal for fear of upsetting the gods. Archaeological investigations have revealed that the "treasure" consists of offerings thrown into the lake, including jewelry, weapons, and body armor. Similarly, ancient Britons deposited high-quality metalwork—much of it deliberately damaged, perhaps to indicate that its function in this world had ended—into Llyn Cerrig Bach on Anglesey, Wales. Although no particular deity is identified with this lake, the votive objects found in its waters are associated with warfare, suggesting

St. Dyfynog's Well, Llanrhaeidr, near Denbigh in Wales. Wells and springs were the sources of clean, unpolluted water and were believed to have medical, religious, and magical qualities. A medieval Welsh poem recounts that St. Dyfynog stood in the cold water of this well as a penance—which explains why its waters were thought to have magical properties.

LEFT **Rivers have long been regarded as the source of life. The names of some Celtic river deities, representing the power of the river itself, are preserved in modern river names such as the Marne (the deity Matrona) in France and the Severn (Sabrina) in Britain. Celtic heroes were believed to meet at a ford in a river to fight or to encounter the sinister "Washer at the Ford," a fairy-woman who washed the clothes of those who were fated to die in the ensuing battle.**

that local aristocrats considered the lake's power influential in their battles. Classical sources suggest that Anglesey was home to an important druid stronghold. Other valuable artifacts recovered from British waters include the famous Battersea shield and the horned helmet recovered at different times from the Thames river in London (see pp.130–31). Their quality suggests that they may even have been made specially as votive offerings, rather than practical weaponry to be borne in battle.

High-status objects such a brooches, shields, and swords were thrown from specially-constructed wooden platforms into Lake Neuchâtel at La Tène in Switzerland. Such objects were not the only offerings deposited at these lake sites—there is evidence of animal and human sacrifice, indicating that the local water-deities sometimes demanded a higher price for their favor.

Among the items offered to water divinities were cauldrons. These prestigious objects had mythological associations—the "Cauldron of Rebirth," which restored the dead to life in the medieval Welsh *Mabinogi*, is said to have emerged from a lake.

BELOW **The gilt-bronze head of Sulis Minerva found at the site of her temple in Bath, England. The head was once helmeted and clearly formed part of an impressive cult statue. Devotees came from all over to bathe in the waters of the shrine at Bath or to sleep in its precincts. Pilgrims dedicated altars to the goddess and deposited inscribed lead plaques—many bearing curses upon wrongdoers or prayers for revenge—in the sacred waters.**

SNOWDONIA, WALES

Areas such as Snowdonia in Gwynedd, north Wales, are the settings for numerous Celtic folk traditions: the deep, mysterious lakes may lead to Otherworld realms, while mountains represent places of sanctuary or the sites of heroic fights with marauding giants. Gwynedd provides the setting for the entire fourth section of the medieval Welsh set of tales, the *Mabinogi*. Centered around the exploits of the brothers Gwydion and Gilfaethwy, nephews of the magician Math, the text tells how Gwydion and Math create a magical wife of flowers called Blodeuwedd for the hero Lleu. Blodeuwedd is unfaithful, and her lover, Gronw, kills Lleu. Gwydion revives Lleu and the two set out for revenge. Blodeuwedd and her maids flee to the mountains. As they look back, they trip and fall into a lake. All are drowned except for Blodeuwedd, who is cursed to spend the rest of her days as an owl—in Welsh folklore, the owl is a bird despised by all others.

THE FISH OF WISDOM

In Irish myth, a certain salmon swam in the Boyne river and was
imbued with great wisdom (salmon represented knowledge), a gift
to be passed on to the first to taste the fish's flesh. Later, the salmon
was caught by the bard Finnegas, who gave it to his apprentice Fionn
Mac Cumhaill to cook. Fionn touched its flesh and acquired magic
powers. Many Celts believed that the sea separated this world from
the next, thus aquatic animals (such as the dolphin image from the
Gundestrup Cauldron, adopted from the Mediterranean world)
became symbols of connection between the two realms.

THE DIVINE FEMALE

Women in Celtic tales were powerful figures, but in Celtic society the position of women was constrained by law. Nevertheless, according to the Peniarth 28 manuscript of Welsh law (from which this image of a woman proffering a dish is taken), women in medieval Wales enjoyed certain social privileges.

Julius Caesar's list of Gaulish deities mentions only one goddess, whom he calls by the Roman name of Minerva. The Romans also gave this name to Sulis, the British goddess who presided over the famous healing springs at Bath in England (see pp. 34–7). However, the role of the Celtic Minerva extended beyond that of a healing goddess, as she was also associated with fertility, good fortune, animal husbandry, hunting, and war. And she certainly was not the only Celtic goddess.

In Celtic belief, the most widely-known female deity was the mother goddess, who represented the rich earth, female fertility, and regeneration. Mother goddesses took many forms. For example, the goddess Aveta was one of several deities worshipped at Trier, the capital of the Treveri in northeastern Gaul. Pilgrims to her shrines left small votive images of a maternal goddess holding symbols of prosperity and plenty such as fruit, lapdogs, and babies.

The complex symbolism of mother goddesses was reinforced by the fact that they were often grouped in threes. Several maternal images found in the Rhineland depict two older goddesses flanking a younger one. In Burgundy, one goddess commonly holds a newborn baby, while two others carry objects such as a piece of cloth or washing implements. Some triple-goddess figures are shown with a spindle, linking the mother goddess with the three Classical Fates, and thus represent the cycle of life, from birth to old age and death.

Other goddesses were portrayed singly, and their functions can often be surmised from their names and attributes. For example, a small Romano-Celtic bronze figure from Berne, Switzerland, shows a goddess offering a basket of fruit to a bear. The goddess's name is Artio, which itself means "bear." The image suggests either that she protected the bears themselves or that she propitiated the animals on

RIGHT The torc around the neck of this figure, who looks out from a panel of the Gundestrup Cauldron, identifies her as a goddess. She is surrounded by birds and smaller figures, perhaps attendants or devotees. One of the birds perches on the goddess's hand while an attendant seems to be braiding her hair.

penkenyð debet hre corium
bouis in hyeme ad faciendu
kynlleuaneu canib; reg. pen
kenyð debet hre iustum dotum ab hebogyð
quolibet festo sancti michaelis. In nono die p
kl nouembr; debet penkenyð cu uenatoribus
ostendere regi canes & cornua cum kynlle
uaneu & pte sua de consil. i. etiam ptem.
Non oportet respondere alicui de causa sui
anti usq; ad nonu die nouebr; pte osin ali
cui de suydogyon curie. Nullus eni de su
ydogyon curie potest perastinare cãm
alicui. si sit qui statim int eos
iudicet. Penk. debet hre ptem
duor miror de consil uenantib;
cum molosis & ab eis qui cum lepo
rariis ptem uni uiri. Unusquisq; de uena
torib; molosor debet hre de consil tantum
qntu duo de uenatorib; leporarior. Penk
debet hre etiam pte a rege de pte sua de
consil. Postqm diuisa fit consil int regem.

& uenatores; penkenyð & uenatores debent
hre chyle sup oms uillanos reg. deinde ad
rege oms ueniant cont natale accepturi
ab eo qd hre debent. i. breyno & deleet.
Locus penk. in aula est; in opposito regis
cont igne sed iuxta columpnam. & cum eo
oms uenatores. Cornu plenu debet a rege
eualind a regina & etium a dysteyn cum
noluerit. Penkenyð i hospitio suo debet
hre ancuyn. s. un lect. cum tb; cornib;.
Ipe debet hre terra ptem de dyruy uenator
& de camlury & de elodyu & de mercede fili
arum illor. Cum rege debent uenatores
ēe a natali sui donec inuenent ceruas
in uere. Crepio cepint uenari in uere usq;
ad nonu die maii; n cogant responde ali
pte osin alic de suydogyon. Venatores & ac
cipitrarii & g wastroyon debent hre chyle
sup oms uillanos reg. semel i anno; sed
singuli separatim.

Camerarius debet hre in docu
menta reg. uncta cum ea reliquerit.

behalf of her devotees, whom she thus protected
from attack. A Gaulish goddess, Sirona, carried the
attribute of a serpent, but this probably means that
she was a healer deity rather than a protector of
snakes—the creatures are a widespread symbol of
healing in the ancient world. Sirona's role as a
curative goddess is confirmed by the fact that
many of her sanctuaries were located at springs.

Numerous Celtic goddesses presided over war
and hunting. A miniature bronze cart from the seventh century BCE, discovered at Strettweg, Austria,
is dominated by a goddess who towers over stags
and shield-bearing horsemen (see illustration,
p.28). A first-century-BCE goddess figure found in
Brittany shows her wearing a helmet with a goose crest—
the goose was a symbol of aggression (see illustration, p.98).

But the most dramatic visualizations of war goddesses are found in
Irish literature and myth. In one famous epic, two grim figures, the
Morrigan ("Phantom Queen") and the goddess Badhbh ("Crow"), confront
the hero Cú Chulainn at the hour of his death. Cú Chulainn had made an
enemy of the Morrigan by refusing her sexual advances. To avenge this
humiliation, the Morrigan, who was believed to know the fate of
warriors in battle, determined that the hero would die in his next
conflict. He was lured into fatal combat by the sorcery of Badhbh, a
war goddess, who hovered over battlefields in the form of a crow. The
Irish descriptions of these two baleful goddesses echo many of the
elements of triplication, transformation, fertility, and aggression that
occur in earlier iconography.

THE "PAPS OF ANU," IRELAND
In Irish tradition a female deity
called Danu was the mother of
the most powerful group of
Irish gods, the *Tuatha Dé
Danann* (the "Children of the
Goddess Danu"). Although she
was originally linked with
rivers, through her association
with the Munster fertility
goddess Anu—which may
simply be another form of the
same goddess's name—Danu
came to be regarded as a
powerful mother goddess
among the Irish Celts,
responsible for the fertility
of all the land in Ireland.
A medieval Irish writer declares
of her: "good was the food she
gave us." Danu/Anu's close ties
with the land gave rise to the
name *De Chich Anann* (the "Paps
[breasts] of Anu") for these two
hills that overlook a valley to
the west of Killarney in
Co. Kerry.

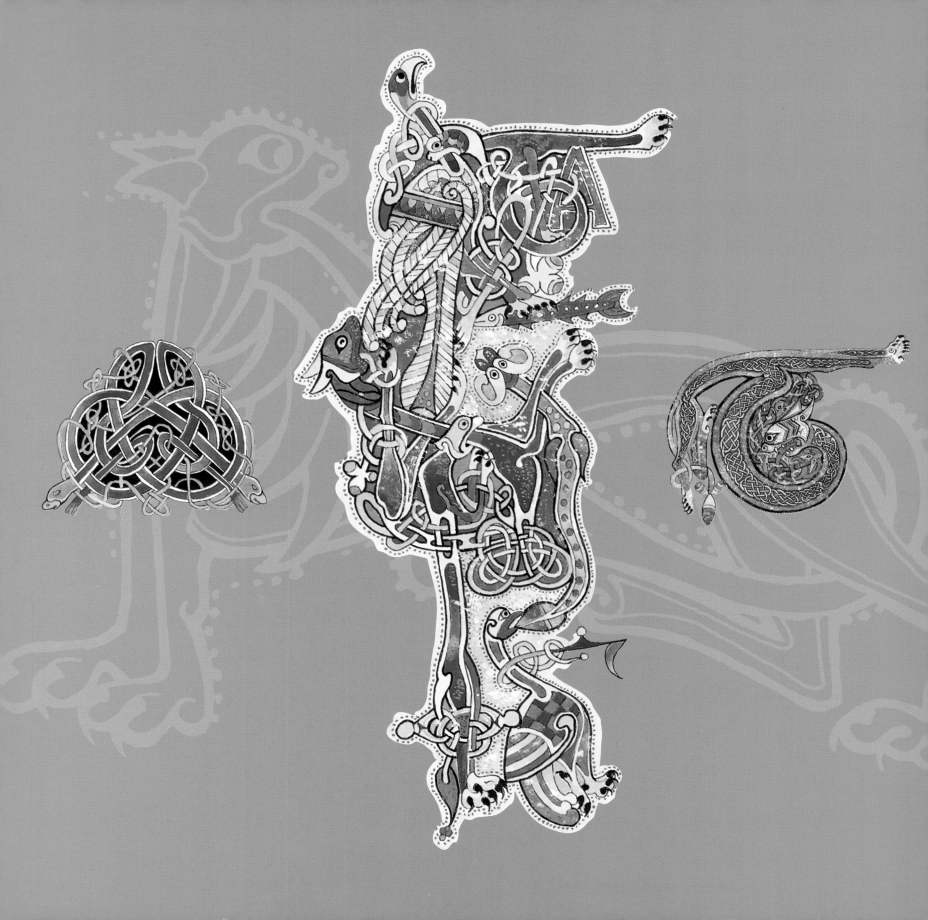

MYTHIC CREATURES

Winged beasts and hybrid creatures appear in Celtic art from its
very beginnings. For example, the antlered deity on the Gundestrup
Cauldron holds a snake with the head of a ram, a curious hybrid
popular in the iconography of northern Gaul. A strikingly powerful
image, the ram's masculine fertility is combined with the snake's
phallic symbolism; and death (because the snake sheds its skin)
is combined with regeneration (the skin's renewal). Most menacing
of all are the carvings of monsters found in the Celto-Ligurian
temples of southern Gaul. In an apparent demonstration of the
triumph of death, these creatures, with huge jaws and clawed feet,
are shown devouring human heads and limbs.

THE SPIRIT OF THE FOREST

According to the Roman poet Lucan (39–65CE), the Celts worshipped blood-thirsty gods in dark woodland sanctuaries. While evidence suggests that this may be a grimly exaggerated description of the truth, the Celts undoubtedly regarded forests and woodlands as sacred places of power and danger.

A widespread Celtic deity that was particularly associated with woods, was the "Horned God," a lord of animals usually depicted with deer-like antlers. Only one representation of this god, dating from the first century CE, gives his Celtic name: Cernunnos, or the "Horned Sacred One." This title, which may have been a local name, is inscribed on a Gallo-Roman altar above a carving of an elderly figure who wears two torcs and has both the antlers and ears of a stag. The altar comes from a sanctuary of the Parisii (see illustration, p.52), a Gaulish tribe, who gave their name to the French capital Paris.

Much older images of the same, or a very similar, deity have been found in other parts of the Celtic world. For example, a horned figure is depicted on a rock carving of the fourth century BCE from Val Camonica in northern Italy, as well as on the famous Gundestrup Cauldron fashioned about a century later (see illustration, right). Cernunnos was linked with prosperity and the abundance of nature, and his close association with the forest-dwelling stag—the god sometimes has hooves as well as deer's ears and antlers—also makes him a symbol of masculine potency. He appears on the Gundestrup Cauldron with the ram-horned snake, a hybrid beast associated with regeneration and fertility. Like the snake, a stag regularly loses and regenerates part of its body:

This stag illustrates a section on hunting in a 13th-century manuscript on Welsh law. Stags were associated with a wide range of Celtic deities, most importantly the horned god Cernunnos (see illustration, opposite).

RIGHT A horned deity from the Gundestrup Cauldron presides over real and mythological creatures as "lord of the animals." His exaggerated antlers link him with the stag that accompanies him, and with the Celtic forest god Cernunnos. The two torcs (one around his neck, the other in his right hand) are a mark of his high status as god, and the ram-headed snake in his left hand suggests that he may also be a god of regeneration.

The name Cernunnos ("Horned Sacred One") is inscribed above the head of this carved deity, found in Paris, France, and dedicated by the "Sailors of the Parisi tribe." A torc hangs off each horn, attesting to the figure's powerful divine status. Stag's ears can just be made out on top of the head, which is unusually bald—Celtic deities tend to be depicted with full heads of hair.

it sheds and regrows its antlers once a year. One recovered statue of Cernunnos has holes for real antlers, which may have been replaced annually by worshippers in a seasonal festival of renewal—perhaps during the spring when new antlers became fully formed. The aristocratic torcs usually worn by Cernunnos indicate his high status, while other attributes, such as food and bags of coins, reinforce his connection with prosperity and well-being.

Cernunnos was probably revered as a god whose power and favor could influence the success of the chase—as the lord of the forest, he was responsible for a great economic resource that provided food, clothing, and fuel. The attribute of a stag in depictions of numerous other hunter deities from woodland regions testifies to the extent and strength of Celtic belief that these gods held power over hunting success. Equally, they protect the animals of the forest, one image shows a deity resting his hand on the antlers of a stag. The seventh-century BCE Strettweg chariot (see p.28) shows a goddess presiding over a hunting party in pursuit of two stags. A Val Camonica rock carving from the same period also depicts a stag hunt. A recovered stag figurine was dedicated to the British god Silvanus Callirius ("Woodland King") at Colchester, England.

Cernunnos was the most prominent horned deity, but there are others who also display an affinity with the natural world, even if they lack Cernunnos' complex attributes. One such deity is thought to have inspired the Medieval Welsh description of a grotesque giant, who summons the animals of the woods by striking a stag so that it bellows. Other gods and goddesses with apparent hunting connections are depicted with hares, another common quarry, or hounds, which were also associated with healing and the Otherworld.

The recovery of votive offerings and cult statues from forest groves and clearings, such as this one in Perthshire, Scotland, attests to the importance of these settings for Celtic sanctuaries and ceremony.

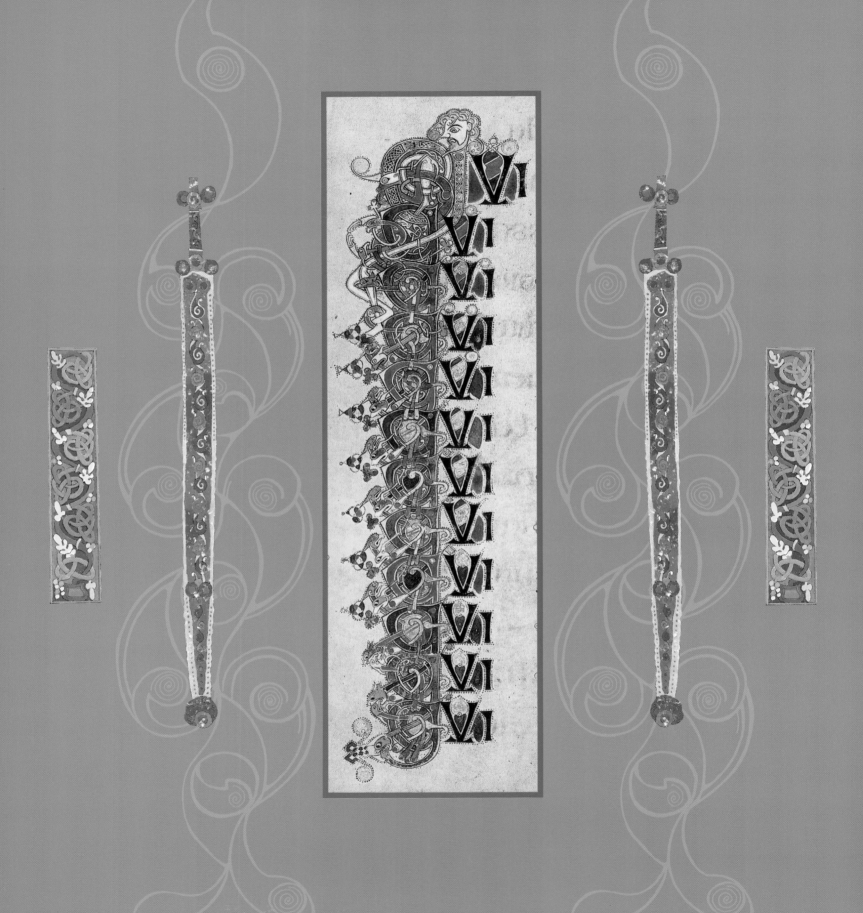

THE TREE OF LIFE

With their tops in the heavens and their roots underground, trees held sacred significance for the Celts. The Tree of Life is found in both pagan and Christian Celtic art. The tree's seasonal cycles linked it with death, rebirth, and growth; its lifespan, with longevity. In Celtic art, the Tree of Life was often a willow, and two Gaulish stone monuments of the 1st century CE show the willow being chopped down by the woodcutter-god Esus ("Good Master"). Esus' symbolic "killing" of the tree affirms the willow's cycle of death and renewal. In the manuscripts and stone crosses of Christian Ireland, under the influence of Byzantine art, the Tree of Life takes the form of twisted vines, representing the resurrection and eternal life of Christ.

THE BLACK FOREST, GERMANY

The sun streaming through the trees of the great Black Forest near Stuttgart, Germany, makes it easy to understand why the Celts considered wooded areas sacred places. Forests played a major role in Celtic religion (see pp.50–53), and at one time the entire Celtic heartlands of southern Germany, like most of northern Europe, probably would have been completely wooded. Some Classical authors described woodland sanctuaries as dark, frightening places that terrified Celtic devotees, who were loath to enter their midst. Woodland sanctuaries with carved wooden images of heads have been found, but Classical authors misjudged the attitude of the Celtic worshippers: many of these sanctuaries were healing shrines to beneficent deities.

FANTASIES OF LEAF AND FLOWER

Leaf, flower, and plant motifs seem to swirl across every surface of Celtic artifacts of the La Tène era. A great array of objects, especially helmets, brooches, and torcs, were incised with leaf and stem designs. According to the Roman historian Pliny the Elder (23–79CE), oak and mistletoe were used in Celtic ritual, but stylized art forms make specific plants hard to identify. Floral patterns persisted into Irish art from the 5th to 12th centuries. Enameled and filigree plant forms decorate fine metalwork made for sacred purposes, and elaborate flower and leaf designs frame manuscript texts.

DIVINE TRINITIES

In Celtic art, three linked "s"-motifs form a pattern known as a triskele. These motifs are common in La Tène design, but continue to appear even in the medieval Christian manuscripts. This bronze disk (1st or 2nd centuries CE) once formed part of a pendant. The arms of its triskele motif spiral out to end with bird-like heads.

One of the most important and recurring elements in the art of the western European Celts was the use of triplication, or groups of three, which may be shown symbolically with threefold patterns or designs, or most significantly and importantly as triple divinities. Celtic deities were often venerated in triple-headed and triple-faced forms—such images intensified the already evocative symbol of the head. Stone carvings that show three heads facing in three different directions have been found as far apart as Ireland and Germany, but the motif was especially prominent around Rheims in France, the ancient center of the Remi, a Gaulish tribe. In this area, the faces of what may be a tribal deity are depicted so that they overlap. This stone carving has only two eyes in total, but the clever design means that each head looks in a different direction and none lacks any facial feature.

We cannot be completely sure of the meaning of such triple-headed figures, but one theory suggests that because the heads look in three directions at once, they may signify the continuity of time (past, present, and future) or the universe (the Earth, the heavens, and the underworld). One of the most important gods to be associated with trinity symbolism was the horned god Cernunnos, who was sometimes linked with figures such as the three-headed Mercury that appears with the horned god on a first-century-CE monument found in Paris. The bull was also a potent symbol, an association that derived from its physical strength. A Celtic image of a bull with three horns is thus particularly evocative.

RIGHT The importance of triads among the Celts is expressed here by a relief of a trio of mother goddesses. The variations in their faces and in the symbols of plenty that they hold, including bread and linen, work harmoniously with the repetition of formal triadic composition.

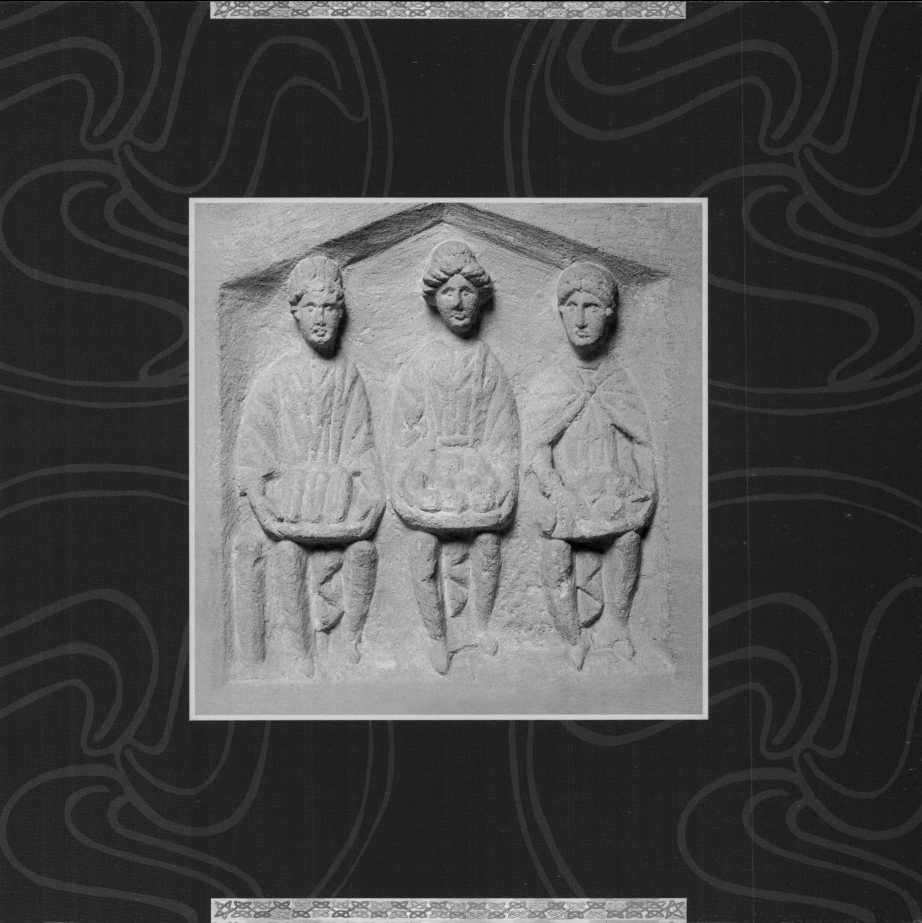

LEFT **This embossed silver horse harness, from Manerbio, northern Italy (2nd–1st centuries BCE), displays potent triplet symbolism. Near-identical heads surround and emphasize a central triskele composed of three Celtic "s"-shaped motifs.**

Three-horned bulls were deposited at Gaulish shrines, and one appears on a ceremonial baton which had been buried with a number of other votive objects at Willingham Fen in Cambridgeshire, England.

Further evidence for the importance of triplication is revealed in the popularity of triplicated mother goddesses. Sometimes all three deities are identical; at other times they each carry different objects. Such triplication would appear either to intensify their overall potency as fertility deities, or else to express three aspects of their maternal role. Images found in Germany tend to show triads of goddesses of different ages, perhaps to express the flow of life from youth to maturity (see also pp.42–5). Britain was home to three small "hooded spirits," the *genii cucullati*, associated with fecundity and renewal, whose images have been found at a number of healing shrines. Although these figures appear elsewhere in the Celtic world, only in Britain have they been found in triplication.

Medieval literature in Ireland, Wales, and other Celtic areas, continued to use triplication, but as a narrative device rather than as a powerful, visual symbol. For example, goddesses and Otherworld beings are sometimes reported to appear in threes moments before a critical or dramatic event. The ancient British bards of the heroic age may have used similar motifs to enliven their narratives. In the first section of the Welsh *Mabinogi* set of tales, King Matholwch, the king of Ireland, describes the maiden Branwen as one of the three "Matriarchs of this Island." Later, there are three Golden Shoemakers, three Noble Youths, and three Unhappy Blows, to name but a few. Similarly, in Irish myth, a hero is believed to know that his death is imminent when he sees three red-headed warriors riding in front of him.

Little figures (*genii*) each wearing a cloak with a hood (*cucullus*) functioned as good-luck charms during the Roman-Celtic period. In Britain they were especially common in the area of Hadrian's Wall, where these *genii cucullati* were found, ca. 1st century CE. Their triplication was no doubt intended to increase their luck-bringing power.

ON WINGS OF DIVINITY

In the medieval Welsh *Mabinogi*, the birds of the Otherworld woman
Rhiannon sing to weary heroes to lull them to sleep. All kinds of
birds are associated with Celtic gods and goddesses in similar ways.
Peaceful and curative doves may have been associated with the god
Mars-Lenus, a healing deity; a goose (known for its aggression and
associated with battle in Celtic symbolism) forms the crest of a war
goddess from Britanny and was sacred to the Britons; and the crow
was associated with Badhbh, a goddess of death. But perhaps the
most powerful bird symbol is the eagle. Associated with the sun god
in pagan Celtic ritual, the eagle was adopted into early Christianity
as the symbol of St. John the Evangelist.

JOURNEYS TO THE OTHERWORLD

Belief in an afterlife was an important aspect of Celtic religion. Sources suggest that there was no conception of reward or punishment after death, but the recklessness of Celtic fighting men led Classical commentators to surmise that the Celts looked forward to being reborn in the afterlife. Although this conclusion can never be verified, the fact that most burials included grave goods does imply that the passage from life to death was viewed as a journey into some sort of new existence for which the dead needed to be prepared. As far as we can glean from later literary sources, the destination of the dead was conceived of as an unearthly, magical region, or Otherworld, which was home also to supernatural beings and monsters. The boundaries of this land were fluid, and all mortals could cross over and enter the Otherworld—at their own risk. At certain important times of seasonal change, however, this flexible frontier was apt to disappear altogether—for example, on Beltaine (May 1) and Samhain (November 1). At these times, the inhabitants of the Otherworld might stalk the mortal region, emerging from the pre-Celtic barrows and other burial sites (see pp.98–99), which were believed to be entrances to the Otherworld.

In Celtic literature, journeys to the Otherworld were an important narrative theme. In Ireland, the realm's inhabitants were known as the *Tuatha Dé Danann* ("People of the Goddess Danu"), who lived in the *Tir na nÓg* ("Land of

This tiny golden boat (late 1st century BCE) with mast, oar, and benches, measures about 2 inches (5cm) from the bottom of the hull to the top of the mast. It was discovered among a hoard of precious objects at Broighter, Co. Derry, in Ireland. Such craft are described in Irish tales of voyages to the Otherworld.

Youth") or the *Tir na mBeo* ("Land of Women"). As death was not a prerequisite for entry into the Otherworld, some stories tell of mortal women being kidnapped as brides for Otherworld men, or of heroes who entered these strange lands and sometimes never returned.

While storytellers often located these mysterious and beautiful worlds within the ancient burial sites, known in Irish as *sidhe* ("fairy mounds"; see p.70), they also envisaged idyllic Otherworld islands beyond great stretches of sea. Examples of these include *Emhain Abhlach* ("Region of Apples") or *Magh Meall* ("Delightful Plain"). Irish tales known as *immrama* describe sea voyages to the Otherworld in which small bands of heroes or holy men visit a series of islands where mysterious

Islands in the Bristol Channel were believed— by the inhabitants of the English and Welsh mainland areas from which they could be seen—to be magical Otherworld realms, blissful places where decay was unknown. Sea mists often obscured these small islands making them seem magically to appear and then disappear.

and symbolic adventures test their intellect and bravery. Some islands are haunted by strange beasts, such as monster cats; some contain springs pouring forth wine, and ever-fruitful trees filled with exotic birds; others are inhabited by beautiful Otherworld women.

The literature and folklore of Wales also record a strong belief in a mystical Otherworld. The medieval collection of Welsh tales known as the *Mabinogi* relate how the hero Pwyll agrees to change places with Arawn, the king of Annwn, the Otherworld. Pwyll's passage into Annwn is aided by King Arawn, who lets him be guided by magical red-eared dogs. The twelfth-century traveler and historian Gerald of Wales told how he had once met a man who, as a boy, had visited a beautiful sunless realm, the inhabitants of which never lied and ate only saffron and milk. However, the young visitor had violated the sacred rules of this magical Otherworld by stealing a golden cup. His punishment was never to be able to find the entrance to the place again.

LEFT **This hound figure (4th century BCE) is the handle of a Celtic adaptation of an Etruscan wine flagon found at Basse-Yutz in the Moselle region of France. Celtic folklore is full of magical hounds, such as the *Cwn Annwn* (the "Hounds of the Otherworld") that accompany the Welsh heroes, or the magical hounds of the *sluagh*, the night-flying fairies found in the tales of Irish and Scottish folklore.**

Many Celtic folktales tell about the search for Otherworld cauldrons. A Classical source mentions a god sleeping on an island attended by nine priestesses whose breath fanned the fire under a magic cauldron. Decorative cauldrons discovered in lakes (such as this one, dating from the 6th century BCE, with a handle in the form of a cow and a calf) may have been used as votive objects.

POULNABRONE, IRELAND
The prehistoric dolmen of
Poulnabrone rises starkly
from the Burren, a rocky
windswept plain in Co.
Clare, Ireland, the earthen
mound that once covered it
long since weathered away.
When the Celts came to
Ireland they found many
such structures—originally
the inner chambers of Stone
Age tombs and perhaps
already more than 1,000
years old. Legends arose
that the huge vertical slabs
surmounted by massive
capstones were gateways to
the Otherworld, an unseen
magical region that lay
beneath, within, alongside,
and beyond the visible
landscape. Irish myth tells
of a divine race, the *Tuatha
Dé Danann* ("Children of
the Goddess Danu") who
retreated through these
stone portals following the
invasion of the Gaels and
founded a new kingdom in
the parallel cosmos. Known
in Irish as *sidhe*, or "fairy
mounds," these entrances to
the Otherworld, of which
Poulnabrone is one, were
also once revered as the
"hostels" of individual
gods and goddesses.

The LIVING BOOK

After the defeat of Gaul, Celtic culture vanished almost entirely from mainland Europe, remaining only in the far West—in the magnificent art and learning of the Christian Celts. St. Patrick's mission established Christianity in Ireland in the fifth century CE, and over the next two centuries the Irish sent out their own missionaries: to Iona and Lindisfarne and even to Switzerland and northern Italy. The missionaries needed tools for their teaching—most importantly, the books of the gospels. Written on fine calf skin, Celtic manuscripts achieved new heights of vividness and intricacy. They were, in the words of one traveler, the work of angels.

LEFT **The first words of St. Matthew's gospel in the Book of Kells, an Irish manuscript of ca. 800CE. The artist devotes most of the page to X (*chi*) and R (*rho*), the first two letters of "Christ" in Greek.**

DESIGN AND DIVINITY

As the Christian faith flourished, Irish monasteries, such as those at Kells, Durrow, and Armagh, became centers for learning and the arts. Missionaries carried the distinctive religious culture of Celtic Ireland to the islands of Iona and Lindisfarne, as well as to other parts of the British Isles and into continental Europe, as far as Bobbio in northern Italy and St. Gall in Switzerland. Despite the disruption caused by the Viking invasions of ca. 700–900CE, this mingling of Christian, Celtic, and Classical civilization, which today is referred to as Insular culture, remained a powerful force in European art and learning.

The great manuscripts, all of which were created within a relatively short period during the seventh and eighth centuries CE, rank among the most outstanding masterpieces of Insular—and indeed European—art. Carefully written and beautifully illustrated, they comprise the four New Testament gospels of Matthew, Mark, Luke, and John in the Latin of the Bible translation known as the Vulgate. Each gospel is preceded by a brief synopsis and a "Canon Table"—a chart identifying parallel passages in the four gospels. Text and decoration are closely integrated with extraordinary sophistication. The illustrative designs draw on both Celtic and Classical tradition. Interlace patterns, often combined with animal forms, recall the spirals and trumpet shapes of La Tène carving, jewelry, and metalwork of around a thousand years earlier, while the colors and forms of animal and human figures may be influenced by those found on Celtic enamel work of the later La Tène period.

Page-space in the manuscripts is mostly devoted to script, but even on the pages that are least illustrated and most heavy with text, small motifs, such as colored dots, small plant shapes, abstract patterns, and interlaced animals, are used

A gilded figure of Christ attached to a book cover from medieval Wales lifts his right hand in blessing and balances a Bible on his left knee. Such elaborate casings protected valuable manuscripts and other precious religious objects.

RIGHT The complex lozenge pattern of this carpet page from the Lindisfarne Gospels (end of the 7th century CE) displays all the elements associated with Irish manuscript art, including interlace, fretwork blocks, and a decorative border. Two small patches to the left, above the cross, remain uncolored, an idiosyncracy of the Lindisfarne scribe who tried deliberately to avoid absolute perfection, so as not to challenge the perfection of God.

The famous mission of St. Patrick firmly established Christianity in Ireland in the 5th century CE. The monasteries developed in a society whose inhabitants were scattered around a rural landscape and bound by ties of family and collective ownership of land. The remote and austere world of the typical Irish monastic settlement fitted well into this arrangement. Boat-shaped oratories, such as the Gallarus Oratory in Dingle, Co. Kerry (the only remaining oratory of its kind left on the Irish mainland), provided a place for prayer and contemplation.

to end sentences and fill in blank spaces. The most complex decoration, however, occurs between major divisions in text. Ornamented initial letters draw the eye to significant passages in the books and are occasionally made up of, or incorporate, images that comment on the meaning of the text. Other elaborate designs enhance the opening words of each gospel by twisting around and through the letters on the page. Portraits of the evangelists and scenes from the life of Christ appear at various points in the text, and there are whole pages of pure decoration, known as "carpet" or "cross-carpet" pages. Even the Canon Tables, which are laid out inside carefully measured columns and arcades, are filled with animals and plant interlacing that transform what are essentially indexes into a style of artistic expression of their own. Whatever sources the artists drew upon, animals and symbols seem to decorate and elucidate the manuscript at almost every turn.

RIGHT **In this page from the Breton Gospel, a central figure is surrounded by the symbols of the four evangelists, all depicted in the act of writing their versions of the gospel story. The border is simple for a manuscript of this type, but the interlaced knots at each corner, decorated with the protruding heads of beasts, are very much in the spirit of Insular manuscript illustration.**

The elaborate use of color in the decoration reflects the artists' astounding ability and mastery in making full use of what we might now consider a very restricted palette. Lapis lazuli from Afghanistan supplied the artists with ultramarine blue, while the distinctive purples and pinks were made from plant dyes. Although it may appear otherwise, there is virtually no gold leaf—the glowing golden color was made from a yellow mineral called orpiment. Tiny holes around the edges of some pages indicate that little pricks along a type of ruler marked out the text and illustration area of each page. Compasses and set squares may have been used to help the artist create the intricate decoration. For the most part, however, the illustration depended on the accuracy of the artist's eye and the steadiness of his hand.

THE ETERNAL KNOT

The eternal knot, tracing an unbroken path without beginning or end, is characteristic of Celtic book decoration. Its origins lie in the plait motifs of the La Tène culture that flourished in western Europe from ca. 500BCE until the first centuries CE. Thereafter, intricate knotwork continued to develop mainly in Ireland, culminating in the interlace patterning that characterizes the manuscripts of the 7th to 9th centuries CE. Exquisite craftsmanship and months of painstaking labor produced ingenious eternal knot designs that can cover entire pages of gospels, psalters, and other religious works. For the pious Irish scribe, the endless knot was a perfect expression of the boundlessness of God and the infinite diversity of his creation.

THE GLORY OF KELLS

In the eleventh century, Irish literary sources record the theft of a precious manuscript of the evangelical gospels of Matthew, Mark, Luke, and John, known as the Gospel of St. Colum Cille (St. Columba). Stolen with it was the gold, bejeweled cover that was both a shrine and a protector for this sacred book. The manuscript, by this time already around three hundred years old, was finally recovered without its gold case. It is known today as the Book of Kells, perhaps the most spectacular of the surviving Insular manuscripts.

The decoration in the Book of Kells epitomizes the artistic qualities of all the Insular texts, but the circumstances in which it was produced are not entirely clear. It may have been fashioned in the monastic scriptorium on the Scottish island of Iona—a mermaid swimming up the center of a genealogy is thought to refer, through a complicated linguistic pun, to Iona and to Columba himself. However, in 795CE, Iona was sacked by the Vikings, and in 807CE, the monks fled and settled instead in Kells. We know that the writing of the book began around the time of the escape to Kells, and it may have been completed there.

At least three scribes and five illustrators worked on the manuscript. Elaborate introductions to the gospel accounts follow portraits of the evangelists themselves, while a number of portrait pages specifically illustrate scenes from the life of Christ (see p.89).

Each of the symbols of the four evangelists from the Book of Kells occupies a different roundel on a page divided by a cross. The spaces surrounding these important religious symbols are filled with myriad details.

The tiny isle of Iona is one of the Inner Hebrides group of islands, and lies off the western coast of Scotland. It measures only about 3 miles (5km) long by little over 1 mile (1.6km) wide. Parts of the Book of Kells were probably written in the island's abbey, but with the onset of the Viking raids, the monks of Iona are believed to have fled with the manuscript to the safety of Kells in Ireland. The grave of St. Colum Cille (who is better known as St. Columba), the book's traditional owner, lies here. The peaceful setting of the abbey today (above) belies its turbulent past.

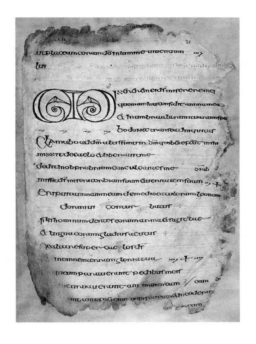

THE SPIRIT OF THE LETTER

Large capital letters, used to mark divisions in the text, provided an opportunity for illustrators to show off their talent and display their artistic flourish. Letters may be filled with bright color, form patterns of interlace, or more magically seem to metamorphose into plant, animal, and even human forms. There are more than 2,000 decorated letters in the Book of Kells alone, and each of them is unique. In many manuscripts, scribes left space among clear and uniform script for decorated letters or illustrations which artists put in later. Where words fell short of a complete line at the end of a paragraph, colorful decoration was often added to fill the space.

MORTALS, SAINTS, AND ANGELS

Magical beasts, never-ending spirals, and ornate representations of nature seem to dominate the Celtic gospel manuscripts. Nevertheless, human figures appear frequently: full-page portraits are offset by figures woven into interlace patterns, contorted into letters, and tucked discreetly into corners. The artists show little concern with anatomical accuracy, often stylizing the human form in order to incorporate a figure into their overall decorative scheme. The Book of Kells contains several groups of men drawn in profile as if they are observing the events being described in the text or illustrated on the page. There are also a number of vignettes showing men that seem to have no purpose or relevance other than to adorn. One small drawing shows a soldier standing on a letter, armed with a sword and buckler, and his foot seems to be caught up in the script. Apparently, his function is purely decorative, as he does not appear to be specifically illustrating any text.

Apart from the Virgin (see illustration, right), few mortal women are depicted in any of the Insular manuscripts. One rare example can be found in the Book of Kells close to a reference to the Old Testament story of Lot: a small face worked into one of the letters on the page may represent Lot's wife. There also seems to be a female face among the ornamentation decorating the account of the women who visit the empty tomb of the risen Christ.

Many of the human figures in the Insular manuscripts are no doubt intended to be representations of the four evangelists. For example, the head and feet that appear above and below St. Matthew's name in the Book of Kells are presumably

LEFT An illumination from the gospel of St. Matthew in the Lindisfarne Gospels (ca. 800 CE). The seated figure is St. Matthew himself, and it is thought that the figure peeking around the curtain may be Christ. The gospels were probably produced by Eadfrith, the Anglo-Saxon Bishop of Lindisfarne.

RIGHT In this full-page illustration from the Book of Kells, Mary, the mother of Christ, is shown cradling her baby son in her arms, while angels appear around them to rejoice at Christ's birth. Mary, apart from being the most prominent female figure to be represented in manuscript illumination, is the only woman who can be identified and named.

In this illumination from the Lichfield Gospels of ca. 720CE, the enthroned figure of St. Mark is identified by the lion that seems to fly above his head. The coloring of the lion's coat recalls the patchwork technique of Celtic enamel work. These gospels were reputedly made for St. Chad by the bishop of Lichfield, England.

intended to depict the evangelist himself. Similarly, in the Book of Kells, the figure who sits at the top of the opening page of Matthew holding a book is surely the author of the gospel with his work. In the corner of the decorated page that opens St. Mark's gospel in the Book of Kells, a lion, the saint's symbol, appears with a man in his mouth: it seems likely that the man, too, represents the evangelist.

In the Book of Kells, the evangelist portraits that precede each gospel are surrounded by interlaced-border and cross-shaped forms, in keeping with the beautiful decorative

style of the entire manuscript. By contrast, the evangelist figures in the Anglo-Celtic Lindisfarne Gospels tend to be more dignified and simple. Even so, they may also be obscure: a mysterious figure, who may be Christ, peers from behind a curtain in the gospel of St. Matthew (see illustration, p.84), and a little head, presumably that of St. John, is incorporated into the first letter of the word *principio* ("beginning") at the opening of this particular saint's gospel.

The style of human figures in the manuscripts is not exclusive to text illumination. A series of statues that now decorate the wall of a romanesque church on White Island, County Fermanagh, Ireland, show saints and bishops with calm and simplified faces just like those in the manuscript illustrations—they may even have been the inspiration for some of the manuscript art. It is thought that the statues were originally carved onto the wall of a ninth- or tenth-century monastery and there is certainly nothing quite like them anywhere else in the art of the Celtic world.

Illustrations of angels abound in the images that show Christ's birth and resurrection—they reflect the joy at these momentous occasions, and are probably based directly on biblical descriptions of the events. Yellow orpiment, which resembles gilding, was used for the angels' hair and wings. Often these angels carry books, flowering wands, or *flabella* (liturgical fans). On one page, a small angel holds open his hands as if in prayer. He is set in the first letter of *omnia* ("all"), a reminder perhaps that the manuscripts were intended for private meditation and public use.

A series of figures, with calm faces such as those in the Insular manuscripts, gaze out from the side of a church on White Island, Co. Fermanagh, Ireland. The figures probably originally decorated an earlier monastery and include a Celtic bishop with his crozier and bell, and Daniel in the lion's den, a popular religious subject.

THE IMAGE OF CHRIST

The Book of Kells is adorned by four stunning full-page images
of Christ: a Madonna and child; the Temptation of Christ in the
wilderness; Christ teaching; and Christ's arrest in Gethsemane. Christ
is also represented by motifs such as the cross of the Passion, a fish (a
Christian symbol that appealed to the Celts, who associated salmon
with wisdom), and the two Greek monograms IHS and the Chi-Rho
(respectively, the first three letters of "Jesus" and the first two of
"Christ" in Greek). Most of these motifs derive from Mediterranean
Christian tradition, but the Irish artist does add some of his own.
Entwined among many initial letters, for example, are two heads,
one old, one young, representing God the Father and God the Son.

HEAVENLY CREATURES

Early Christian tradition regarded a variety of creatures as symbols
or embodiments of Christ and the evangelists. Given the Celts' own
associations between divinity and metamorphosis (see pp.94–7), the
Irish manuscript artists took to this tradition with enthusiasm. For
example, the flesh of the peacock was said to be incorruptible, and
so the bird came to represent the eternal, resurrected Christ.
Similarly, the early Church associated the gospel writers with
celestial creatures that appear in the Bible. Matthew was symbolized
by a man or an angel, but the other evangelists were all animals:
a lion for Mark; an ox for Luke; and an eagle for John.

IMAGE, BELIEF, AND RITUAL

LEFT Soon after 400BCE, waves of Celtic warriors invaded the Po Valley in northern Italy. The area became known to the Romans as *Gallia Cisalpina* ("Gaul on this side of the Alps"; see map, p.11). From this newly occupied territory, Celtic art and beliefs spread to other parts of the Italian peninsula.

Much of the Celtic cultural legacy—whether imagery on ancient artifacts or in medieval literature—suggests that the Celts, in both pagan and Christian times, recognized no clear distinction between the realities of this world and the features of the supernatural. In ancient Celtic religion, a complex system of rites sought to uphold the delicate harmony between gods and people. Christianity brought a radically different mode of belief with new forms of ritual, but for several centuries the new faith was to maintain a distinctly Celtic outlook, expressed most memorably in the handiwork of the gospel-book artists of Ireland.

BELOW This carved head once reinforced the handle of a 1st-century-BCE bucket found in Kent, England. Celtic art frequently combined important ritual images, such as the head, with practicality.

MAGIC AND METAMORPHOSIS

In a poem attributed to the semi-mythical Welsh poet Taliesin, the bard declares, "I have been in many shapes before." Metamorphosis, the ability to change shape or form, is a prominent motif in many Celtic tales, and examples are also to be found in Celtic art. The deer-like characteristics of the god Cernunnos—antlers and hooves—certainly suggest that shapeshifting between the animal and human worlds was believed possible, but images of this deity are among the handful of Celtic artifacts that actually attest to this. Other images imply a welding of human and animal essences rather than forms, as in the Gaulish statue of a war god who bears the image of a boar, a symbol of war and hunting, as an attribute (see illustration, opposite).

The interest in magical transformation among the Celts may be rooted in a feeling for the fluidity of the cosmos—the malleability of the boundaries between this world and the next. Movement between the mortal world and the Otherworld was thought to take place at certain special times of year. In Irish myth, the hero Oengus assumed the form of a swan to follow his lover into the Otherworld on the feast of Samhain, when the barriers between the two realms were at their most fluid (see pp.98–9).

Rebirth into a new life through metamorphosis is also touched upon in the tale of Oengus. The hero's brother Midir was unable to resist falling in love with the beautiful maiden Étaín. This brought on the wrath of Midir's first wife, who, in a fit of jealousy,

The fantastic Celtic imagery of a human-headed horse, with the wildly flying hair of a Celtic warrior was developed for the reverse of Celtic coins from the standard image of the horse and chariot on ancient Greek coinage. This example comes from the Le Mans region of France.

transformed Étaín into a huge red fly. Oengus took pity on the girl and partly undid the magic by allowing her to return to human form each night after dark. But the wife was not satisfied with this, and one day sent a strong wind to blow the fly into the wilderness. After many years, Étaín fell into a cup of wine and was swallowed. This allowed her to be reborn as a beautiful maid. When eventually Midir found her again, Étaín was the wife of the king of Ireland and oblivious to her previous life. By tricking the king into letting him kiss Étaín, Midir reminded the girl of her past life and she fell in love with him again. Both turned into swans and flew away to Midir's home.

As the stories of Oengus, Midir, and Étaín illustrate, birds were frequently the result of human transformation in Celtic belief. Another tale relates how the Children of Lir were magically transformed into swans by their wicked stepmother and sang in the Otherworld. Images of a carrion bird perched on the back of a horse, which appear on Iron Age coins from Brittany, may reflect Celtic tradition known from Ireland in which battle goddesses assume the form of crows and ravens, particularly at the time of a warrior's death. The Irish war goddesses may also appear as beautiful young women or ugly hags—they take on their hideous aspect after they have been wronged in some way.

In some accounts, supernatural beings assume the forms of animals. The set of Irish tales known as the Fenian cycle is rich with examples of transformation. The divine wife of the Irish hero Fionn (see p.40) and the mother of his son Oisín, first appears to her husband as a fawn, having been transformed as punishment for failing to fall in love with a druid. Fionn's aunt was briefly turned into a dog, during

A stone image of a Gaulish god, found at Euffigneix, Haute-Marne, France, and thought to date from the 1st or 2nd centuries BCE. The presence of the torc around the neck identifies the figure as a deity—probably of nature. The boar impression in its right side indicates that the essences of the god and the animal were believed to be inseparable.

which time she gave birth to a canine son, who later became one of Fionn's trusted hounds. In the Welsh *Mabinogi* tales, a magical woman who plagues heroes (the wife of *Llwyd Cil Coed*, the "Gray Man of the Wood"), takes the form of a mouse to conduct her torment.

Welsh legend abounds in accounts of magical shapeshifting. In one story, magicians create a beautiful woman, Blodeuwedd, out of flowers. However, she later proves unfaithful (see p. 38), so the magicians punish her by turning her into an owl, believed to be a creature of the evil forces of darkness. Another tale recounts how Lleu, a Welsh hero, turns into an eagle after being struck with a spear, but recovers his human form through the care of his magician uncle. Culhwch, another hero, must face a giant boar (a transformed king who would not mend his evil ways) in order to retrieve a comb, scissors, and a razor so that the father of his bride-to-be may groom himself for the wedding.

According to some scholars, these shapeshifting and magical motifs may indicate a Celtic belief in regeneration and the afterlife, which was envisaged as a more perfect version of ordinary life. It is certainly true that many Celtic deities were believed to have a specific regenerative function: divine attributes such as fruit and grain imply fecundity, while animals such as snakes (which shed their skins several times a year to reveal new growth underneath) and deer (which annually shed their antlers and grow new ones) may also imply an association with the cycle of death and rebirth.

This wide-eyed animal head, probably a bull, is a bronze mount from a 3rd-century-BCE wooden wine flask found at Brno-Malomerice in the Czech Republic. Animals were often the result of metamorphosis in Celtic myth.

The spirit of Celtic illumination underwent a revival when scholars in Renaissance Wales began to speculate about the history of their Celtic ancestors. In this manuscript illustration of 1594, the interlace letters and metamorphic imagery vividly recall Celtic art. The page shows the Greek myth of Actaeon, a hunter who is turned into a stag by the goddess Artemis, and is then set upon by his own hounds.

A YEAR OF FESTIVALS

This bronze figure from Dineault in Brittany, France (1st century CE), depicts a warrior goddess in a crested helmet. She resembles Classical statues of Athene, the goddess of healing. In Irish tales, warrior deities such as this may visit the real world at Samhain.

Early Irish literature records the names of four great seasonal festivals that marked important divisions in the Celtic year. The summer began at Beltaine (thought to mean "Great Fire") on May 1, and winter began at Samhain ("End of Summer") on November 1. The two other festivals, closely linked to specific deities, were Lughnasa, the feast of the god Lugh, celebrated on August 1 as a traditional harvest festival; and Imbolg (thought to mean "Sheep's Milk"), which fell on February 2. Imbolg was under the protection of the goddess Brighid and, later, her Christian successor, St. Bridget; her festival celebrated the beginning of spring and the birth of lambs and other livestock.

A Gaulish calendar discovered at Coligny, near Lyons, in France, at the end of the nineteenth century, and thought to originate from the first century BCE (see illustration, right), is a remarkable record of the old Gaulish language as well as of Celtic timekeeping. The calendar covers sixty-two lunar months with two intercalary ("leap") months to keep the lunar calendar in line with the solar year and ensure that the festivals always fell in the correct season. It specifically names Samhain (spelled *Samonios* on the calendar itself) as the beginning of the Celtic year. All the Celtic festivals began on the eve of the specific day of celebration.

The four seasonal festivals reflect the pastoral and agricultural cycles of the year, but they were also magical times when the boundaries between the real and supernatural worlds were believed to be at their weakest. In Welsh tradition, the eve of Beltaine (*Calan Mai*, "May Eve") was the night when the magician-poet Taliesin was rescued from the river by his foster father, and the night that Pryderi, a hero of the *Mabinogi* tales, was stolen as a baby from his mother Rhiannon.

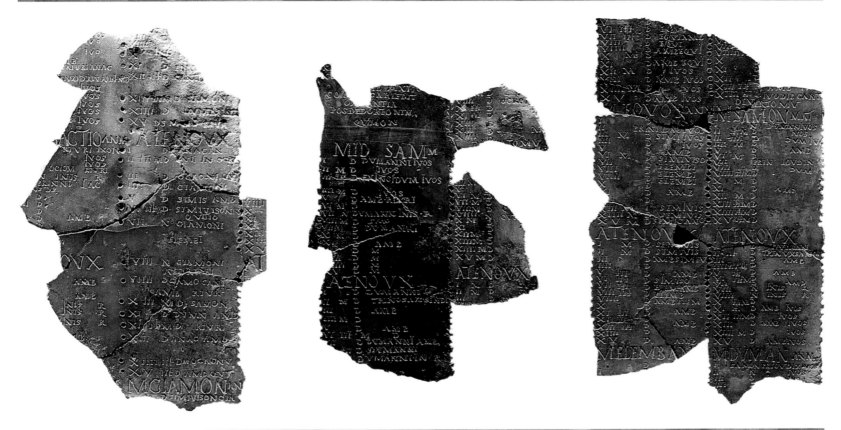

The best-known Celtic celebration of all was Samhain (this is the Irish and Gaelic name for the festival—it is *Calan Gaeaf*, "Winter's Eve," in Wales). Many of the key events in Irish mythology, such as the arrival of the mystical *Tuatha Dé Danann* people (see p.70), took place at Samhain, when the boundaries of this world and the supernatural realm were believed to dissolve completely, and the *sidhe* (fairy) mounds, where the people of the Otherworld lived, were open. In one Irish tale, the hero Neara Mac Niadhain ventured out one Samhain night to pursue an army of *sidhe* people who had invaded his country. He knew that, on this night, they would be unable to close the entrances of their fairy-mounds against him.

The Coligny calendar (1st century BCE) was found in fragments, apparently the result of ritual damage rather than age. Three of the pieces are shown here. The language on the calendar is Gaulish, written in the Roman alphabet. The calendar may have been used to calculate the times of ceremonies.

GRIANAN AILEACH, IRELAND
The exceptionally well-preserved stone ringfort at Grianan Aileach in Co. Donegal, Ireland, dates in part to the 5th century BCE. In prehistoric times, the site was defended by four concentric ramparts and may have provided a center for tribal power and trade. It is also thought that the ramparts may have been used as enclosures of sacred space—primitive open-air temples. The boundaries may represent those between this world and the next. Such prehistoric Celtic hillfort structures were brilliant engineering achievements that exploited the natural terrain for defensive purposes. The high walls would have been an impressive outward sign of political power. The quarrying and movement of the stone to construct the fortifications was itself an extraordinary feat.

SACRIFICE AND CEREMONY

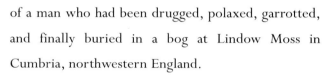

These four male heads (2nd century BCE), discovered at Entremont in France, may have been part of a temple dedicated to a cult of the warrior-hero. Classical authors feared the Celts as headhunters, but this fear may have derived from the existence of such monuments rather than actual practice.

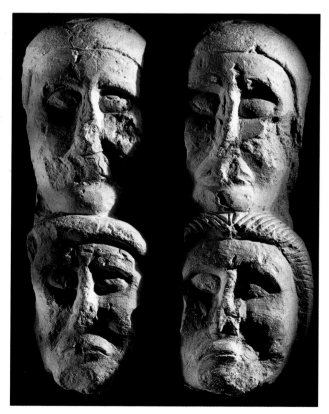

According to Greek and Roman observers, Celtic sacrificial practices were dramatic and bloody. Celtic priests allegedly stabbed victims and predicted the future from their death throes, or burned captives alive in huge wicker figures. It was said that victims sacrificed to the god Esus were stabbed and hanged in trees until they bled to death. Tacitus claimed that the altars of the druids in a sacred grove on the isle of Anglesey, Wales, were drenched with blood and festooned with entrails. Although such accounts are likely to be colored with Classical prejudice and are probably exaggerated, archaeologists have uncovered a number of abnormal burials of individuals who may have been sacrificed. This is certainly true in the case of a man who had been drugged, polaxed, garrotted, and finally buried in a bog at Lindow Moss in Cumbria, northwestern England.

Animal sacrifice appears to have been particularly associated with funeral rites. One important individual was buried in Yorkshire, England, alongside several of his horses. The bones of some geese—a bird associated with the Celtic Otherworld—have been found in graves in Slovakia.

Modern archaeology provides substantial evidence for Celtic burial rituals. For example, evidence of funeral feasting has been uncovered in several of the Celtic graves at Hochdorf in southwestern Germany. But in terms of major ceremony, the installation of a king was particularly important, because the sacred link between the ruler and the land was evidently

central to Celtic kingship and remained so into medieval times. In Ireland, a ritual called the *tarbfheiss* ("bull sleep"), in which a white bull was slaughtered, confirmed the acceptance of the High King and his sovereignty as Ruler (see p.108). Writing in the twelfth century, Gerald of Wales describes a ritual in which a white mare was slaughtered and boiled in broth at the inauguration of an Irish High King, who bathed in the broth and feasted on the horseflesh.

Victory in battle, too, was marked with its own ritual sacrifice. The Celtic victors would slaughter captured animals and dedicate them in thanks to the gods.

Imperial Rome usually respected the religion of conquered Celtic peoples, and ceremonies were long allowed to continue at sites such as this at Glanum, in southern France, an important Gaulish healing shrine.

KEEPERS OF WISDOM

W riting was a relatively late innovation in Celtic society, and so, for centuries, the spoken word was the chief method of maintaining Celtic culture. The principles of law, myth, and religion were upheld by being repeated from one person to another until the time that manuscripts began to appear. Those who were responsible for upholding, fostering, and adding to this body of wisdom were the bards, druids, and seers of ancient Celtic society. While the druids were later supplanted by Roman power, the importance of poets, prophets, lawyers, and storytellers continued in Celtic society until well after the Middle Ages.

The Greek author Strabo and the Roman general Julius Caesar, among other Classical observers, give long accounts of the role of the druids, who commanded the utmost respect among the Celts because they were the supreme guardians of the sacred lore. Their area of expertise covered divination and prophecy, as well as the supervision of religious activities, such as ritual sacrifice at sacred lakes and groves. Celtic metalwork recovered from Llyn Cerrig Bach in Anglesey, Wales, suggests that the site was a druid sanctuary, perhaps even the one referred to by the Roman historian Tacitus as the scene of the druids' last stand against the Roman invaders of Britain. Druidic importance, however, was not only with regard to superstition and religious belief. Druids were also required to memorize long and complex law codes and to give judgments on legal cases.

The importance of music in Celtic society is recorded in statues such as this of a god playing a lyre (from Côtes D'Armor, France; ca. 70BCE). Bards and druids would use music to help them to remember the complex poems, legal lists, and matters of religion that were central to Celtic society.

RIGHT Honor was paramount in medieval Wales, and law tracts give detailed accounts of the penalties for *sarhaed* ("insult"). This illustration from a 13th-century manuscript of Welsh law shows one man pulling another's hair—a serious offense against the second man's personal honor.

BELOW This bronze headdress (ca. 50CE), which may have been a priest's or druid's crown, was found in a Romano-Celtic temple in Norfolk, England. Its precise function is unknown.

cum equo quo castrum regis edificent:
interim erunt ad expensam regis.
Mabeþ ilth cuyrnostauc reddat mi
nistris reg. xii. s. cu singlis domit ne
uictus eius dissipent horreis.

Houem sunt membra homi
nis principalia .i.
duo oculi. duo labia. due
manus duo pedes. nasus. quoy quodq.
sex uaccas & sex uncias argenti. & suo

Although all Celtic societies must have had some sort of priestly class, the druids themselves were apparently found only in the British Isles and Gaul. Artifacts believed to be associated with druid activities include a group of bronze head-dresses discovered at a Romano-Celtic temple built in Norfolk, England, during the second century CE; similar objects are known from Ireland. For example, four carefully crafted bronze trumpets, decorated with typical La Tène patterning and perhaps used in druid ceremonies, were found in a lake near Navan Fort, County Armagh, an important Irish Iron Age stronghold.

After the decline of Roman power in Britain and Gaul, the learned classes were dependent on the patronage of a native aristocracy for their survival. There is ample evidence for a complex system of poets and patrons in Scotland, Wales, and Brittany, which continued in some areas until the seventeenth century. According to Irish tradition, the bards and *filidh* (poets) took over the role of the druids. As well as these learned orators, Ireland had a special class of lawyers, whose job it was to interpret the intricacies of the ancient Irish legal system. Medieval Welsh law tracts, such as the Peniarth 28 lawcode, give specific details about the duties and privileges of numerous types of bards.

In ancient times, Celtic keepers of wisdom undoubtedly had to have exceptional memory skills in order to store all the religious law, divination, prophecy, mythology, poetry, and songs that they were required to accumulate. According to some Classical sources, including Strabo and Caesar, it took a druid up to twenty years to learn everything he or she had to know—all without the aid of writing. Even in later centuries, story-telling from memory was a prized skill. In one medieval Welsh tale, a character called Gwydion vab Don is said to be the best storyteller in the world, but, like a bard or a druid, he is also a great magician and a shapeshifter.

LEFT **Woodland areas and certain trees such as beech, willow, and oak were especially sacred to the Celts. In a series of Welsh poems, the legendary prophet Merlin is driven from civilization into the dangerous world of the dark woods by his own madness. There he addresses an apple tree, his only source of food, wisdom, and inspiration.**

BELOW **This harpist adorns a silver-covered reliquary of the 7th to 8th centuries CE. His high status is indicated by the long hair and flowing robes that characterized Irish nobility in the early medieval period. The harpist's role combined the function of entertainer with that of historian.**

PORTENTS AND PROPHECIES

The Celts frequently left votive offerings at sacred wells. These could be quite elaborate objects to indicate the specific favor required: perhaps models of eyes for better sight, and of arms or legs for greater strength. At Madron Well in Penzance, Cornwall, England, people continue to this day to leave pieces of colored rag tied to bushes as tokens of their wishes.

The druids were intermediaries between the natural and the divine worlds. They were believed to possess supernatural powers that enabled them to peer into the future and to predict the best times for battles, harvests, royal inaugurations, and other events in Celtic life. It was undoubtedly druids who determined which periods of the year were considered "good" (*mat*) or "bad" (*anmat*), as recorded in the first-century-CE Gaulish calendar found at Coligny, France (see pp.98–9).

Divination came in various forms. A simple method might be to watch the way that a bird flew through the sky, while on a more complex level divination might take place as part of an elaborate ritual, such as the ancient *tarbhfeiss*, or "bull feast," that inaugurated the reign of the High Kings of Ireland. When a new king was to be chosen, a druid would consume the flesh and blood of a sacrificed bull and then wrap himself in the beast's flayed skin. He then fell into a profound sleep during which he would learn the identity of the next High King.

This Romano-Celtic pewter mask is thought to represent a priest or a god. The holes along the top of the mask suggest that it is votive object that was at one time attached to another surface, such as a wall. The mask was discovered in a culvert near the ancient springs at Bath, England.

The Celts associated, many Bronze Age burial mounds with the power of prophecy. Anyone brave enough to sleep on such a mound would wake up next morning either a poet or a madman. The twelfth-century historian Gerald of Wales promotes a similar method of inherited prophecy in Welsh lore when he describes seers who gained their insights after lapsing into a trance-like sleep. Coinneach Odhar (d. 1577), a celebrated prophet, also called Brahan Seer, is said to have gained his divinatory powers during such a sleep. Similar practices are reported on the remote Western Isles of Scotland as late as the eighteenth century.

ADORNMENTS AND AMULETS

High-ranking women were often buried with rich jewelry, including bracelets, beads, decorative hairpins, and earrings. The 6th-century-BCE earring shown here, found in a grave at Hallstatt in Austria, is made of beaten and embossed gold.

The ancient Celts clearly so adored finery that they must have presented a bizarre spectacle to their more restrained neighbors in the Classical world. Diodorus of Sicily, a Greek historian of the first century BCE, made a point of noting the Celtic fondness for brightly colored clothes adorned with rich embroidered designs, or else woven patterns that were "striped … with close checks of various colors"—in other words, tartan. In contrast to the short-haired and clean-shaven men of Greece and Rome, who wore simple tunics, Celtic men sported trousers, long hair, and, in the case of the nobility, great drooping moustaches. Some tribes bleached their hair with lime water and wore it spiked. A fierce group of peoples based in Scotland were nicknamed *Picti* (meaning "Painted Ones") by the Romans, probably on account of their tattoos or body-paint.

Striking clothes and hairstyles were complemented by magnificent jewelry of superb handiwork fashioned in bronze, silver, and gold and found all over the former Celtic world. Diodorus was struck by the fashion, among both men and women, for wearing "bracelets on their wrists and arms, heavy gold solid necklaces around their necks, enormous rings, and even golden corselets." Decorated fibulae (sprung pins) and brooches were essential for keeping in place the high-quality woolen clothing.

The heavy "necklace" referred to by Diodorus is the Celtic neck-ring, known today as the torc. Many finely wrought examples have been found in graves, at shrines, and also in buried hoards of treasure (most notably

RIGHT Large tubular torcs, such as this one of the 1st century BCE found at Camp de Mailly, near Reims in France, were made of gold-wrapped iron in order to conserve gold. Their massive size suggests that they were ceremonial or perhaps used to adorn certain cult statues.

A bronze crescent-moon fibula (a sprung-pin brooch used to fasten clothes), found in a Hallstatt grave and thought to date from the 6th century BCE. Embossed pendants hang from the boat-like central piece upon which sit two animals, possibly stylized birds (boats and birds were both Otherworld symbols). The body of the "boat" is decorated with circular emblems, thought to represent the sun.

those dating from around the first century BCE), where they would have been placed during times of danger as amulets to invoke the power and protection of the gods.

Torcs were linked to aristocratic or divine status. One magnificent example, thought to date from the sixth century BCE, was found in the lavish grave of a high-ranking woman at Vix in Burgundy, France. Classical authors describe Celtic warriors in battle as naked except for their most valued possessions—their weapons and torcs. The British queen Boudicca, or Boadicea, who led a revolt against the Romans in eastern England in 60CE, is said to have worn a torc of twisted gold.

This round filigreed bronze fibula was found at Dürrnberg, near Salzburg in Austria, and is typical of the Hallstatt period (ca. 800BCE–ca. 500BCE).

As well as being magnificent items of jewelry and symbols of status, torcs were probably worn as amulets to invoke divine power and protection. There are numerous images of Celtic deities depicted wearing these necklaces—symbols of their importance among the Celtic gods and goddesses. The horned god Cernunnos (see pp.50–53) typically has a single torc around his neck and clasps another in his hand. The presence of two neck-rings suggests that he was a highly revered god. A statue of a veiled woman from a healing shrine at Chaumalières, near Dijon in France, who may be a pilgrim, a priestess, or even perhaps the goddess of the shrine herself, is depicted wearing just one torc.

Discoveries of hoards of elaborate jewelry, including items such as this silver torc, found at Chao de Lamas, in northeastern Spain, have enabled scholars to trace the expansion of Celtic influence in Iberia during the 7th to 8th centuries BCE.

TREASURES OF THE LORD

The peaceful setting for St. Kevin's church, Glendalough, Co. Wicklow, Ireland, is appropriate to the gentle nature of the saint, who loved animals. A medieval manuscript by Gerald of Wales illustrates St. Kevin surrounded by many kinds of birds and beasts.

As the Christian faith became established in Ireland, founding monastic communities developed into busy religious, intellectual, and artistic centers. Even during the Viking raids (ca. 795–950CE), monasteries remained steadfast focal points of Irish ecclesiastical culture. From the seventh century CE onward, contact between the Irish monasteries and those of Britain and mainland Europe produced an elaborate artistic style that represented a remarkable mix of Irish, British, Anglo-Saxon, Pictish, and continental elements. Patronage encouraged the production of a wide range of items: altar vessels and *flabella* (liturgical fans); reliquaries, portable

shrines containing the relics of saints, including their books and bells; croziers (hooked staffs) for bishops; and, of course, sacred manuscripts—small and comparatively plain volumes for teaching, and large, exuberantly decorated books, such as the Book of Kells (see pp.80–81), for liturgical use. These treasures were usually commissioned by the churches and monasteries themselves, or else by secular patrons who sought ecclesiastical support or divine favor.

Reliquaries containing the bones of holy men and women, or their special possessions (such as books or hand bells), were carried throughout the country from one religious establishment to another. Some reliquaries were actually shaped like the rectangular Irish churches or houses of the period. Perhaps the most famous of these is the so-called "Monymusk" reliquary, thought to be from Scotland and dating from the seventh or eighth centuries CE. It is made of wood and decorated with silver and silver-gilt. Reliquaries tended to be embellished with biblical scenes as well as interlaced animals, abstract designs, and even figures playing the harp. The precious hand bell that reputedly belonged to St. Patrick, Ireland's patron, was kept carefully protected in a beautiful shrine that still exists (see p.116). Carvings on churches (see illustration, p.87) and stone crosses depict bishops holding such bells, which would have been rung to indicate the times of prayer. Bishops were also usually shown carrying a crozier, the symbol of their office. Magnificent croziers were adorned with plaques of bronze, silver, and occasionally

The Cross of Cong was commissioned by Tulough O'Connor, King of Connaught, around 1120CE to enshrine a sacred relic. A master craftsman named Maél Isu U Echan created this magnificent piece which reflects both the uniqueness and the adaptability of Celtic art. The cross is a wonderful example of gilt bronze openwork and enamel decoration.

enamel, which in turn would be decorated with interlaced animals or foliage. Often a small reliquary box was built into the crook.

The beauties of such rich artifacts were not lost on the invading Vikings. To the horror of Irish Christians, the pagan marauders would discard the holy relics and tear up the exquisitely illustrated books containing the word of God in order to steal only the valuable casings that protected them. Portable shrines were transformed by the raiders into jewelry caskets, and the gilt bronze fittings of religious vessels were turned into brooches for Viking women.

Sacred books were often believed to have important talismanic properties—for example, the Book of Durrow was allegedly dipped into sacred water so that any ailing person who later touched it might be cured of their disease—and they were often kept in elaborate covers, known as *cumtach* (book shrines). The stolen cover for the Book of Kells was probably one such book shrine. A *cumtach* was often adorned with an elaborate bronze or silver plaque (see illustration, p.74) depicting Christ extending his hand in blessing, the Crucifixion, or the four evangelists.

The Irish ecclesiastical gold, silver, and bronzework of the eighth and ninth centuries, and some popular motifs such as spiral and trumpet patterns, can be found to have their roots in earlier La Tène designs. The decoration of altar vessels, such as the eighth-century Ardagh chalice, with its interlacing and inlays of reddish enamel, appears to have continued the tradition of La Tène artistry—its glories now marshaled in the service of God.

LEFT The beauty of St. Patrick's Bell shrine reflects the preeminence of the saint in Celtic Christianity. The bells of the saints were important relics, and so were protected by special shrines or cases. Usually, however, the reliquaries would have been simpler in design than this.

Tall, round towers such as this one at Narrow Water Castle, Co. Down, have been variously interpreted as defensive fortifications, watchtowers, and places to house the sacred bells that called the monks to worship. Whatever their function, they symbolize the continued uniqueness of Celtic culture in Ireland on the eve of Anglo-Norman incursion.

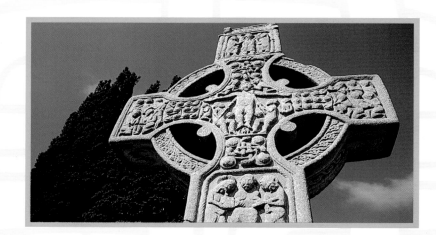

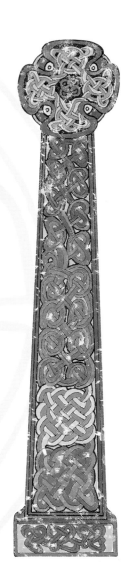

THE CROSS OF LIFE

The characteristically Celtic cross developed from the simple Chi-Rho monogram of Christ. The leg of rho became the stick of the cross, while the "x"-shaped chi moved up the leg and became a straight crossbar encircled by the round head of the rho. From the 8th century on, stone crosses in this form became important in Irish monastic sculpture. Sculptors filled in the main cross with animal interlace and curvilinear decorations. Irish annals sometimes refer to such crosses as *cross an screaptra* ("cross of the Scriptures"), presumably because they depicted Bible stories, although the term *cross aird* ("high cross") was more popular. Over time, decoration became more elaborate, culminating in the spectacular high crosses of the 10th century with their intricate depictions of gospel stories.

the immortal hero

LEFT This bronze warrior head was recovered from a Celtic chariot dating from the 1st century BCE at Dejbjerg on the southwestern coast of Denmark. The symmetry, staring eyes, and long moustache are typical of the period.

A combination of skill and almost supernatural bravery characterized the cult of the hero among Celtic societies. A Celtic delegation to Alexander the Great claimed that they were afraid of nothing except that the sky might fall in on them. This proud statement of fearlessness affirms the opinion of the Greeks and Romans that Celtic warriors displayed a level of bravery that bordered on recklessness. For centuries, such boldness held together an empirical Celtic power—in life, the warriors were the political mainstay; after death, their graves became the focus of ritual activity and their deeds lived on in songs, poetry, and tales.

BELOW A medieval copy of the Welsh *Cyfraith Hywel Dda* ("The Laws of Hywel the Good") depicts a *rhingyll* (a "sergeant-at-arms"), an important official. He wields a spear, the symbol of his office.

A PEOPLE AT WAR

The Greek historian Strabo (ca. 64BCE–ca. 21CE) declared that the Celts were, quite simply, "war mad." They would fight purely for the sake of fighting, which meant fighting among themselves if no other enemy presented itself. While archaeological findings have revealed a complex people who were pastoralists, farmers, and keen traders, the cult of the warrior was undoubtedly central to Celtic society. Three richly furnished tombs, discovered in Germany and dating from ca. 800–ca. 500BCE, emphasize the importance of the warrior class. At Hirschlanden near Stuttgart, a statue of a warrior with a dagger, and wearing a torc and a conical hat, dominated an aristocratic burial mound (see illustration, p.132). An apparently important male, also with a dagger, torc, and headgear, was buried in a tomb near Hochdorf in Baden-Württemberg, together with other richly ornamented weapons and elaborately decorated hunting gear. More recently, in 1996, a magnificent warrior statue, believed to date from ca. 500BCE, was discovered near Glauberg, northeast of Frankfurt. The statue—perhaps the best-preserved Celtic sculpture ever found—is thought to show a Celtic prince wearing armor and a carved torc about his neck. The six-foot statue may once have towered over the prince's grave.

Combat provided an arena where personal, tribal, and family alliances could be tested, strengthened, or destroyed. Military skills might be kept honed by carrying out cattle-rustling raids on non-allied neighbors, a practice suggested by several Irish tales, notably the *Táin Bó Cuailnge* ("The Cattle Raid of Cooley"). These tales

The sword, dagger, spear, and shield in this Welsh lawcode indicate that the art of war was as important to the medieval Welsh as it was to their Celtic forebears. The lawcodes are very specific about how the weapons should be crafted.

RIGHT This bronze belt plaque from Slovenia (ca. 5th century BCE) shows a Celtic warrior wielding a lethal axe as he marches into battle. The artist has exploited one of the studs in the plaque to give the warrior's shield a large central boss.

The Celts practiced the art of fighting with implements resembling
dumbells. The two figures on this bronze situla from Slovenia
(ca. 5th century BCE) are engaged in such combat. In the Welsh
narratives, heroes are said to have fought together every May Day
until the end of time for the hand of a beautiful woman.

point to a society where courage and fighting skills were paramount. Such values were upheld by a military aristocracy whose structure was maintained through an elaborate system of fosterage: noble children were raised outside their immediate family circle and were trained by experienced fighters in the arts of war.

Great attention has been devoted to the Celts' apparent interest in headhunting, which has given rise to the understanding that, for the Celts, the head was the most important and powerful part of the body, rather than, say, the heart, which was held in the highest esteem by other cultures. Strabo describes a Celtic custom of decapitating dead enemies and keeping the heads kept as trophies, but there is no conclusive evidence to suggest that the rites he records were practiced by all Celtic tribes. Nevertheless, the abundance of artifacts in the form of busts, triplicated heads, and skulls, recovered from all over the Celtic world, does attest to the head's trans-Celtic function as an important symbol of power. In the sanctuary at the ancient capital of the Saluvii tribe, Entremont, near Aix-en-Provence, France, human skulls had been placed in niches, and the statuary of the shrine included limestone sculptures of warriors (or gods) sitting cross-legged behind piles of human heads (see illustration, p.102). The discoveries at Entremont, and similar finds at nearby Glanum and Roquepertuse, suggest that this area was home to a distinctive local cult. There are no traces of sacrifice at these shrines, but the prominence given to severed human heads suggests that they may have been dedicated to some aspect of a warrior cult.

RIGHT This warrior-deity, made of embossed sheet bronze with glass eyes, was found at the Celtic sanctuary at St. Maur en Chaussée in southern France, and dates from around the 1st century BCE. His hairstyle resembles the hair on the piles of carved heads at Roquepertuse (see main text).

DUN AENGUS, IRELAND

The spectacular Irish hillfort of Dun Aengus is dramatically situated on the edge of a vertical cliff overlooking the Atlantic Ocean on the west coast of the island of Inishmore, in Galway Bay. It dates from the 1st to 5th centuries CE and, like all ancient hillforts, exploits the natural environment for defensive purposes. The large enclosure (which would have housed people—including craftsmen and the local chieftan—and animals) is defended by a zone of up to around 70 feet (23m) wide of densely packed limestone pillars. These were rammed into the limestone bedrock either diagonally pointing outward, or upright. We might assume that their function was to slow down the approaching enemy, whether on foot or on horseback, by making access through to the main fortress walls painful and slow. A single, narrow passage leads through this defensive stone forest to the outer and inner walls, each of which today stands to a height of 12 feet (4m)—we can only guess at their height when they were first completed. The innermost of these walls seems impenetrable: accessible only through very narrow gaps in the outer wall, it is as thick as it is high. In Celtic tales, hillforts are often the setting for heroic adventures—in such stories, the forts are depicted as being populated by fearsome monsters, and the defensive pillars are flaming barriers or rings of stakes topped with human heads.

THE FACE OF THE WARRIOR

The head, as the center of the self, was a potent symbol among the Celts. It was not surprising that artists of the time created such numerous images of faces. The warrior class favored drooping moustaches and heavy torcs worn around the neck. The carved head shown above illustrates these attributes, although the long moustache has been stylized to create a symbolic spiral at either end. Further insight into warrior appearance comes from Classical sources, which describe Celtic warriors as fair-haired, sometimes with hair bleached lighter still with limewater. These men were arrogant and hot-tempered, cultivating war whenever they could.

ARMS AND ARMOR

Given the importance of warriors and warfare to ancient Celtic society, it comes as no surprise that Celtic artisans often lavished as much skill on their weapons as they did on jewelry and other luxuries. Smiths who could forge bronze and (from the eighth century BCE) iron into military equipment were no doubt accorded high status. Although they never developed the technology for casting iron, the weapons that the Celts produced by heating and hammering were nonetheless innovative and, above all, deadly.

By the La Tène period, Celtic smiths had perfected a heavy slashing sword with a long flat double-edged blade that could be used by horsemen and footsoldiers alike. Shields were also long—often oval or rectangular in shape (see illustration, left). Miniature versions of these shields are commonly found in graves, in which they were placed so that they may protect the soul after death, as well as being discovered at cult sites, where they were offered to the gods in return for strength and protection.

Shields were wielded by a single central handle, with a projecting boss (pommel) on the other side to protect the hand. Sometimes this boss was extended into a narrow spine that ran down the center of the front of the shield, strengthening it and thus affording further protection to the arm and hand. Eventually, Celtic smiths developed the ability to form the boss and handle out of one piece of metal, thus making the whole shield more sturdy. The magnificent bronze

LEFT This ceremonial shield, dating from the 1st century CE, was found in the Thames river at Battersea, London, England. The symmetrical, deceptively simple layout, composed of raised curves and red glass inlays, is typical of the British-influenced La Tène style.

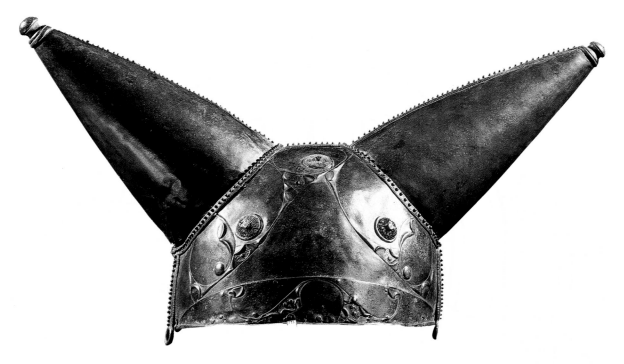

shields that have been found in Britain and elsewhere were no doubt for ceremonial or display purposes only—the shields taken into battle were probably made mainly of wood, covered with leather and painted. The ceremonial specimens were highly decorated, the front of the shield filled with scenes of battle, defeated captives, wrestlers, stylized animal forms, and abstract patterns. The pommel, a grip, and a guard were enriched with enameling, and the grip was often hammered into a beautiful stylized figure, to create a perfect fusion of function and design.

Other pieces of armor included helmets and chain-mail shirts. Classical writers give detailed descriptions of Celtic bronze helmets with elaborate decoration showing birds and animals. Few examples survive but, like the decorative shields, these helmets were probably for ceremony only and not intended to be worn in combat. However, much simpler bronze and iron headgear, more suited to practical use, have also been discovered. Only the most gifted metalsmiths made the Celts' iron chain-mail shirts (literally loops of iron linked together to form a sort of mesh)—and probably only the warrior aristocracy could afford to buy them.

The horns and pattern of raised studs and swirling La Tène designs on this impressive bronze helmet, suggest that the headgear was used for ceremony rather than as actual battle armor. It dates from the 1st century CE and was found on the banks of the Thames river in London, beneath Waterloo Bridge. Like the Battersea shield (see opposite), it may have been thrown into the river as a votive offering.

In the middle Danube area, swordsmiths produced spears and daggers that were highly decorated with animals, leaf and flower shapes, and with mystical beasts such as dragons, but again, like the elaborately designed helmets and shields, these weapons were probably used for ceremonial purposes only. More simple designs, dating from around the second and first centuries BCE, have been recovered in significant numbers from sites in Switzerland, but these may reflect the changing artistic styles, which simplified the decoration of weaponry, rather than any more practical use.

Armor aside, the Celts employed some other, highly imaginative forms of protection. The Greek author Diodorus of Sicily records an object known as a *carnyx*. This was an animal-headed war trumpet "of a peculiarly barbaric kind … which produces a harsh sound to suit the tumult of war." Examples of these instruments with horses' heads are depicted on the third-century-BCE Gundestrup Cauldron (see illustration, p.134), while a boar's head, broken off from the top of a *carnyx* and dating from ca. 50CE, was discovered at Deskford in Grampian, Scotland. As we have seen, war for the Celts afforded warriors the opportunity for personal displays of valor and prestige, and the *carnyx* played an important role in the build-up to battle. Producing a kind of prolonged scream, intended to send shivers of fear through the waiting opponent, the *carnyx* provided a background sound to the riotous clamor of the warriors, who shouted boasting taunts, sang battle songs, and made ritual displays of aggression in a terrifying frenzy before the onset of battle.

Bronze phalerae often formed part of horse harnesses or were used to decorate warrior-chariots. This example, found in a Gaulish warrior-grave in the Marne, northeastern France, would have once had intricate openwork patterning around its circumference.

This sandstone figure from Germany (6th century BCE) is more than 3 feet (1m) tall—unusually large for Celtic art. He is naked except for a torc and conical hat, and a dagger that can just be seen beneath his right hand.

Ireland is home to a number of archaic defensive sites known as
ringforts. This image of the Grianan of Aileach ringfort displays the
sturdiness of the outer walls even today. Although many of the
structures on these sites are medieval buildings, they recall the
spirit of the Otherworld dwellings so prominent in folktales.

DIVINE STEEDS

A procession of mounted warriors feature prominently in this mythic scene depicted on the silver-gilt Gundestrup Cauldron of ca. 3rd century BCE, discovered in Denmark.

The horse played a vital role in both Celtic society and religion. Celtic warriors used horses to pull chariots and for cavalry duty; hunters used them to gain speed in the chase; devotees made offerings of horse sculptures to war gods, such as the Gaulish god Rudobius; and Celtic kings stamped their coins with the image of a horse in preference to the eagles, lions, and griffins of other ancient powers. As well as being an emblem of royalty and prestige, the animal represented sexual prowess and fertility, and was also associated with the life-giving powers of the sun. In Roman times, horses appeared atop soaring columns as the celestial mount of the Celtic sky god, who trampled the monstrous forces of darkness.

Horses were linked with a number of other gods and goddesses, of whom the most popular was Epona, a mother-goddess figure (see pp.42–5) whose name means simply "horse goddess." Her cult was widespread and deeply rooted among the ancient Celts, and in the Roman period she became the only Celtic deity to be honored with a festival at Rome (December 18). Epona was often depicted riding on a mare, perhaps accompanied by a foal, dispensing the earth's bounty of bread, grain, or fruit; or she might appear bearing a key and followed by a human figure, an image believed to represent the souls of the dead being conducted to the gates of the Otherworld. She protected horses and their riders: one riding master dedicated an altar to her to protect his pupils.

Memories of this ancient goddess survived in the tales recited centuries later by the bards of Christian Wales and Ireland, which feature women on horseback with magical associations. Welsh legend, recorded in the *Mabinogi*, tells of the mysterious Otherworld woman Rhiannon, whose male pursuers cannot catch up with her sauntering white horse no matter how fast they gallop. In Irish myth, Niamh, a fairy-woman with golden hair, bears the warrior Oisín off to the Otherworld, where the pair are married. If Oisín ever desires to visit his home again, and yet retain his Otherworld immortality, he must ride there on horseback and never allow his own feet to touch Irish soil.

A stylized representation of a horse's head of ca. 75CE from Yorkshire, England. This elegant bronze piece would have been attached to the frame of a chariot.

PRONUNCIATION GUIDE

Irish

a – hard as in l*a*ss, or long as in dr*a*wn

ae, ao – long as in p*a*y

ai – "*ee*" as in s*ee*n, or "*ah*" as in f*a*ther

bh – "*v*" as in *v*ictory

ch – before or after e or i, as the "*f*" sound made by "*gh*" as in cou*gh*; or before or after a, o, or u, as the "*ch*" sound in the Scottish word lo*ch*

dh – a hard "*th*" sound, as in *th*is

e, ea, ei – short as in b*e*t, or "*ay*" as in p*a*y

gh – before or after a, o, or u, like the "*g*" in the Spanish word a*g*ua, but like a "*y*" (as in *y*ellow) before or after an e or an i.

i – short as in p*i*t, or as the sound "*ee*" in s*ee*n

ll – like the "*gl*" in the Italian word *gl*i

mh – "*v*" as in *v*ictory

oi – as a short "*o*" as in p*o*p, or as "*aw*" in dr*aw*n

Welsh

ai, ei, eu – as a long "*i*" sound as in w*i*re

ch – long as in the Scottish word lo*ch*

dd – as the hard "*th*" in *th*en

f – "*v*" as in *v*ictory

ff – a soft "*f*" as in *f*our

i – "*ee*" as in s*ee*n, or else short as the "*i*" of p*i*t

ll – with a heavy breath behind it, similar to the sound of "*hl*"

oe – "*oy*" as in b*oy*

rh – with a heavy breath behind it, similar to the sound of "*hr*"

u – a short "*i*" sound as in p*i*t, or else "*ee*" as in s*ee*n

w – open as "*w*" in w*i*re, or else as "*oo*" in r*oo*t

GLOSSARY

enameling Applying a glossy layer of color to metal, which is then fixed by firing, for decorative purposes.

fibula A type of pin or brooch, used by the Celts to fasten together items of clothing.

filigree patterning Strictly, the ornamental lacework used to decorate usually precious metals such as silver and gold. The term is sometimes applied to patterning that imitates true filigree.

Gallia Cisalpina "Gaul on this side of the Alps"—the name given to the part of northern Italy occupied by the Celts.

gilding Placing a layer of gold leaf or golden color over another metal, usually silver or bronze.

Hallstatt culture The name applied to the culture (ca. 800BCE–ca. 500BCE) spanning the late Bronze Age and early Iron Age in Europe. It is sometimes considered the first truly "Celtic" culture.

La Tène culture The name applied to an archaeological culture found in much of Europe and the British Isles ca. 300BCE–ca. 50BCE. The artistic style associated with it is closely bound up with Celtic culture.

millefiore Intricate flower-like patterns made from bunches of glass rods fused together, then sliced and used as inlays in metalwork.

phalera A disk, usually ornamental, that often formed part of a horse harness or chariot.

votive object An object offered to a deity by a devotee to gain that god's or goddess's favor or to fulfil a vow.

FURTHER READING

Backhouse, Janet. *The Lindisfarne Gospels*, British Library Press, London, 1995

Bain, George. *Celtic Art: Methods of Construction*, McClellan, Glasgow, 1951

Brown, Peter. *The Book of Kells*, Thames & Hudson, New York and London, 1980

Chadwick, Nora. *The Druids*, University of Wales Press, Cardiff, 1997

——. *The Celts*, Penguin Books, New York and Harmondsworth (England), 1971

Chapman, Malcolm. *The Celts: the Construction of a Myth*, St. Martin's Press, New York, and Macmillan Press, London, 1992

Cross, T.P. and Slover, C.H. *Ancient Irish Tales*, Barnes and Noble, New York, 1969

Cunliffe, Barry. *The Celtic World*, McGraw Hill, New York, 1979

——. *The Ancient Celts*, Oxford University Press, New York and London, 1997

Curtin, Jeremiah. *Myths and Folk Tales of Ireland*, Dover Publications, New York, 1975

Davies, Sioned and Jones, Nerys Ann. *The Horse in Celtic Culture: Medieval Welsh Perspectives*, University of Wales Press, Cardiff, 1997

Dillon, Miles. *The Cycles of the Kings*, Chicago University Press, Chicago, 1948

Dillon, Miles and Chadwick, Nora. *The Celtic Realms*, Cardinal, London, 1973

Dudley, D.R. and Webster, G. *The Rebellion of Boudicca*, Routledge, New York and London, 1962

Ehrenberg, Margaret. *Women in Prehistory*, British Museum Press, London, 1989

Eluere, Christine. *The Celts: First Masters of Europe*, Abrams, New York, 1993

Filip, Jan. *Celtic Civilisation and its Heritage*, Collet's, Wellingborough (England), and Academia, Prague, 1977

Fox, Robin Lane. *Pagans and Christians*, Penguin Books, New York and London, 1986

Galliou, Peter and Jones, Michael. *The Bretons*, Blackwell Publishing, Cambridge (Massachusetts) and Oxford, 1991

Gantz, Jeffrey. *Early Irish Myths and Sagas*, Penguin Books, New York and London, 1981

—— (trns.). *Mabinogion*, Penguin Books, New York and Harmondsworth (England), 1976

Green, Miranda. *Symbol and Image in Celtic Religious Art*, Routledge, New York and London, 1989

——. *Exploring the World of the Druids*, Thames & Hudson, New York and London, 1997

——. *Dictionary of Celtic Myth and Legend*, Thames & Hudson, New York and London, 1997

——. *The Celtic World*, Routledge, New York and London, 1995

——. *Celtic Goddesses: Warriors, Virgins and Mothers*, British Museum Press, London, 1995

Henderson, G. *From Durrow to Kells: the Insular Gospel Books 650–800*, Thames & Hudson, New York and London, 1987

Henry, Françoise. *The Book of Kells*, Thames & Hudson, New York and London, 1974

——. *Irish Art of the Early Christian Period*, Methuen, London, 1965

——. *Irish Art During the Viking Invasions*, Methuen, London, 1967

Hutton, Ronald. *The Pagan Religions of the Ancient British Isles*, Blackwell, Cambridge (Massachusetts) and Oxford, 1991

Hyde, Douglas. *Beside the Fire: Irish Folktales*, Irish Academy Press, Dublin, 1978

Jackson, K.H. *A Celtic Miscellany*, Penguin Books, Harmondsworth (England), 1971

Jacobs, Joseph. *Celtic Fairy Tales*, Bracken, London, 1991

James, Simon. *Exploring the World of the Celts*, Thames & Hudson, New York and London, 1993

Joyce, P.W. *Old Celtic Romances*, Talbot Press, Dublin, 1961

Kinsella, Thomas. *The Táin*, Oxford University Press, New York and London, 1970

Kruta, V., Frey, O., Raftery, B., and Szabo, M. *The Celts*, Thames & Hudson, New York and London, 1985

Laing, Lloyd. *Celtic Britain*, Granada, London, 1981

Laing, Lloyd and Laing, Jennifer. *Celtic Britain and Ireland AD 200–800: the Myth of the Dark Ages*, Dublin Academy Press, Dublin, 1990

——. *Art of the Celts*, Thames & Hudson, New York and London, 1992

——. *The Picts and the Scots*, Dover Publications, New

York, 1993

Lover, Samuel and Crofton Croker, T. *Ireland: Myths and Legends*, Senate, London, 1995

MacCana, Proinsias. *Celtic Mythology*, Chancellor Press, London, 1983

Meehan, Aiden. *Celtic Design: a Beginner's Guide*, Thames & Hudson, New York and London, 1991

—. *Celtic Design: Animal Patterns*, Thames & Hudson, New York and London, 1992

Meehan, Bernard. *The Book of Durrow: a Medieval Masterpiece at Trinity College Dublin*, Dublin Town House, Dublin, 1995

Megaw, Ruth and Megaw, Vincent. *Celtic Art from its Beginnings to the Book of Kells*, Thames & Hudson, New York and London, 1989

Nash, D. *Coinage in the Celtic World*, Seaby, London, 1987

O'Kelly, Michael. *Early Ireland*, Cambridge University Press, New York and Cambridge (England), 1989

Owen, A.L. *The Famous Druids: a Survey of Three Centuries of English Literature on the Druids*, Oxford University Press, New York and Oxford, 1997

Peiler, R. *The Celtic Sword*, Oxford University Press, New York and Oxford, 1993

Piggott, Stewart. *Ancient Britons and the Antiquarian Imagination: Ideas from the Renaissance to the Regency*, Thames & Hudson, New York and London, 1989

—. *The Druids*, Thames & Hudson, New York and London, 1985

Powell, T.G.E. *The Celts*, Thames & Hudson, New York and London, 1980

Raftery, Barry. *Pagan Celtic Ireland: the Enigma of the Iron Age*, Thames & Hudson, New York and London, 1997

—. *Celtic Art*, Routledge, New York, and UNESCO/Flammarion Press, Paris, 1996

Rankin, H.D. *The Celts and the Classical World* Routledge, New York and London, 1996

Rednap, Mark. *The Christian Celts: Treasures of Late-Celtic Wales*, National Museum of Wales, Cardiff, 1991

Rees, Alwyn and Rees, Brinley. *Celtic Heritage*, Thames & Hudson, New York and London, 1961

Ritchie, W. and Ritchie, J. *Celtic Warriors*, Shire Archaeology 41, Aylesbury, 1985

Ross, Anne. *Pagan Celtic Britain: Studies in Iconography and Tradition*, Constable, London, 1992

Sharkey, John. *Celtic Mysteries*, Thames & Hudson, New York and London, 1975

Stead, I.M. *Celtic Art in Britain before the Roman Conquest*, British Museum Press, London, 1996

Stead, I.M., Bourke, J.B., and Bothwell, D. *Lindow Man: the Body in the Bog*, British Museum Press, London, 1986

Thomas, Charles. *Celtic Britain*, Thames & Hudson, New York and London, 1997

Woodward, A. *Shrines and Sacrifice*, Batsford/English Heritage, London, 1992

Youngs, Susan. *The Work of Angels: Masterpieces of Celtic Metalwork*, British Museum Press, London, 1989.

Zaczek, Iain. *Chronicles of the Celts*, Past Times Publications, London, 1996

INDEX

Page references to main text are in roman type; page references to captions are in **bold** type.

A

Actaeon, legend of **97**
Alesia, Roman/Celt battle site 13
angels, manuscript decoration 87
apple tree **107**
Ardagh chalice 117
armor **122**, 130–32, **132**
  decorated 18, 21, 27, 122, 130–32
  ritual offerings **34**, 35, 37, **131**
arms 121, **122**, 130–32, **132**
artistic techniques
  crosses, stone 21, **118**
  curvilinear style 9, 14, 18, **23**
  enameling 21, **53**, **59**, 131
  filigree metalwork **14**, **59**
  geometric designs 18, **18**
  of Insular culture 74, **77**, 80, 84, 114
  interlacing 18, **79**, **97**
  knotwork **79**
  leaf and stem designs **59**

manuscript techniques *see* manuscript decoration
metalwork 18, 19–21, **53**, 130–32
nature-based designs 9, 14, 27, **59**
openwork **14**
patronage 21
shield decoration 131
spiral patterns 14, **23**, 84
sculpture 86–7, **87**, 122, **132**
art symbols
  adaption of Classical symbolism **14**
  metamorphosis 94
  mythical beasts **49**
  religious symbolism **90**
  symbolic significance 21
  Tree of Life **55**

B

bards 104, **104**, 106
Bath, sacred hot springs
  head of Medusa **32**
  head of Sulis Minerva **37**

sanctuary of Sulis Minerva 34, 42
  votive offerings **108**
Battersea Shield 37, **130**
beads **107**
beech tree **107**
bell shrines **117**
belt clasps **12**
belt plaques **122**
Beltaine festival 66, 98
birds **113**
  associated with deities **42**, **64**
  subjects of metamorphosis 95, 96
  war goddesses 45, **64**, **98**
Black Forest, Germany **56**
boar 94, **95**, 96
Book of Kells **73**, 80, **80**, **81**, **83**, 84, **84**, 86, 89, 117
  see also manuscript decoration
book shrines **116**, 117
Boudicca (Boadicea), British queen 113
bracelets **110**
bravery 8, 121
Breton Gospel **77**
brooches **13**, **14**
bulls 60–63, **96**, 103, 108

tarbfheiss (bull-sleep) 103, 108
burial mounds (barrows)
  Celtic 10, 122
  pre-Celtic 66, 67, 99

C

Caesar, Julius, Roman general 28, 42, 104, 106
Calan Gaeaf see Samhain
Calan Mai see Beltaine
calendar *see* Coligny calendar
calf **69**
Canon Tables 74, 77
carnyces see war trumpets
Castell Henllys, Celtic round houses (reconstructed) **16**
Catuvellauni tribe 14
Cauldron of Rebirth 37
cauldrons, decorated **8**, **24**, **28**, **44**, **69**
  offerings to water deities 37, **69**
  see also Gundestrup Cauldron
Celtic civilization
  extent of 9, 10, **113**
  law 42, **45**, 104, 106, 107, **108**, 121

Celtic culture (overview) 8–9, 10–13, 106
  see also bards; druids; religion
Celtic society
  military aristocracy 37, 125
  princely ruling class 10, 21
  social and religious customs 9
Cernunnos ("Horned Sacred One") 50–52, **50**, **52**, 60, 94
  depicted with torcs 113
Chad, St. **86**
chariots **19**, **28**, 52, **121**, **132**, **135**
Chi-Rho **73**, **89**, **118**
Christ, images of **75**, **84**, **89**, **90**
  monograms of **89**
  see also Chi-Rho
Christianity
  Irish missionary activity 74
  new belief system 93
  St. Patrick 73, **76**
circular motifs 112
clothing 21, **45**, 110
coinage 14, **14**, **94**, 95
Coinneach Odhar, prophet 108
Coligny calendar 24, **25**, **99**
Colum Cille, St. 80, **81**
cow **69**

crosses
  Cross of Cong **115**
  development of Celtic form **118**
  stone 21, **118**
cumtachs see book shrines
Cunobelinos, ruler of Catuvellauni 14

D

daggers 122, **122**, **132**
Delphi, attacked by Celts 13, 28
Diodorus of Sicily, Greek historian 110–13, 132
disks *see phalerae*
divination 108
  from human sacrifices 102
  see also druids
druids 37, 104
  bronze headdresses **104**, 106
  memory of 106
  oral transmission of culture 106
  prediction of future 102, 104, 108
  ritual sacrifices 102, 104
  sanctuary in Anglesey 102, 104
  trumpets 106
"dumbells," fighting with **124**
Dun Aengus hillfort **126**
Dyfynog, St. **35**

E

Eadfrith, bishop of Lindisfarne **84**
earrings **110**
Entremont, Saluvi capital and shrine 125
evangelists, four 74, 80, **80**, 84–7, **90**

F

fairies
  Irish **70**, 99, 135
  Welsh **69**
festivals 98–9
fibulae (sprung pins) 110, **112**, **113**
Fionn, Irish mythical hero **40**, 95–6
fish of wisdom **40**, **89**
flabella (liturgical fans) 87, 114
flagon (wine jug) **7**, **31**, **69**
flower designs **59**
  see also plant motifs

G

Gallarus Oratory, Dingle **76**
Gallo-Roman period **9**
genii cucullati (hooded figures) 63, **63**

Gaulish (language) 24, **25**, 98, **99**
Gerald of Wales, traveler/historian 69, 103, 108, **114**
Glanum, France 125
goddesses
  Anu **46**
  Arduinna 32
  Artio 42
  Aveta 42
  Badhbh 45, **64**
  Belesama **25**
  Bóinn 34
  Brighid 98
  Danu **46**, 66–7, **70**, 99
  Epona **45**, 135
  Matrona 34, **37**
  Medusa **32**
  Minerva 42
  Morrigan 45
  Rosmerta 31
  Sabrina **37**
  Sequana 34
  Sirona 45
  Sulis Minerva 34, **37**, 42
  triplication of 45, **60**, 63
  of war and hunting 45, **64**, 95, **98**
gods
  Belenus 34

"Mercury" 28–31, 60
Cernunnos 50–52, **50**, **52**, 60,
    94, 113
Esus **55**, 102
horned forest deities 50, **50**
Lugos 31
Mars Lenus 31, **64**
multifunctional 31
of nature **9**, **24**, **95**
Silvanus Callirius ("Woodland
    King") 52
Taranis **31**
gold 13, 14, **14**, 18, **23**, **107**, **110**,
    117
boat **66**
iron wrapped in **107**
see also jewelry
gorgon **32**
gospel books
    Breton **77**
    Kells see Book of Kells
    Lichfield **86**
    Lindisfarne see Lindisfarne
      Gospels
    see also manuscript decoration
Grianan Aileach ringfort **100**,
    133
Gundestrup Cauldron **8**, **24**, **40**,
    42, **49**, 50, **50**, 132, **134**

H

Hadrian's Wall **63**
hairpins **107**
Hallstatt, Austria **7**, **18**
    graves 10, **28**, **110**, **112**
    salt deposits **7**, 10
Hallstatt period (first Celtic phase)
    10, **14**, 18, **34**, **113**
hand bells **115**
harpists **107**
headgear 122, **132**
    see also helmets
heads, symbolic importance of
    7, **28**, **31**, 60, **93**, **113**, **102**,
    121, 125, **125**, **128**
    decapitation of captives **102**
    triplication of 60, **63**, 125
helmets **12**, 37, **59**
    decorated **98**, 131, **131**
high crosses **118**
hillforts 10, 106, **126**
horse harnesses (phalerae) **18**, **21**,
    19, **21**, **63**, **132**
horses **18**, **21**, 134–5, **135**
    cavalry 134, 135
    human-headed **94**
    importance in Celtic culture 21
hounds **28**, **69**, 96, **97**
houses 16

I

Imbolg festival 98
Iona 73, 74, 80, **81**
Ireland 8, 9, 13
    bull sacrifice (tarbfheiss) 103
    Celtic crosses, development of
    118
    law 106
    manuscript decoration 21, 73,
    74, **74**, 77, **89**, **90**
    see also individual manuscripts
    monasteries 74, **76**, 86–7, **87**
    mythology 94–9
    Ogham script 24
    ringforts **133**
Iron Age society 10

J

jewelry 14, 18, 21, 27, 110, 113,
    113
    bracelets **110**
    brooches **14**, 18, 21, 37, **59**,
    110
    earrings **110**
    symbolism **112**
    see also torcs
Jupiter see Taranis

K

Kells, Book of see Book of Kells
Kevin, St. **114**
    church of **114**
kings
    divining the High King 103, 108
    of the Catuvellauni tribe 14
knot designs **79**

L

La Tène style 9, 12, **14**, 18–23, 74,
    79, 106, **131**
    animal motifs 18
    body shields **13**, 21, 130
    fluidity of form **23**
    influence on Christian artifacts
    117
    plant motifs 18, **59**
    symbolism 21
La Tène, Switzerland 13, 32
    lake offerings 37
lakes **27**, **34**, 35, **38**, 104
law **42**, **45**, **104**, 106, **121**
    oral transmission of 104, **104**,
    107, **108**
leaf shapes **59**
    see also plant motifs
letters, decorative **83**

Lichfield Gospels **86**

Lindisfarne Gospels 73, **74**, **84**, 86

literature 66–9, **69**, **107**, 121

Irish 94–6, 98, 99

magic hounds **69**

triplication in 63

Welsh *see Mabinogi*

Lough Conn, Co. Mayo **33**

Lucan, Roman poet 50

Lughnasa festival 98

M

Mabinogi, Welsh set of folk tales **38**, 63, **64**, 69, 96, 98, 135

manuscript decoration 21, 27, **59**, 74–7, **79**, 80, **90**, 115

angels 87

Book of Kells 80, **80**, **81**, **83**, 84, 86, **89**, 117

Breton Gospels **77**

color in 74, 77

compass decoration 77

Lichfield Gospels 86

Lindisfarne Gospels 73, **74**, **84**, 86

human figures in 84–7

lettering 77, **83**

techniques 77

Marne river **37**

megalithic monuments (dolmens), gateway to Otherworld **70**

Merlin (prophet) **107**

metamorphosis (shapeshifting) 9

animals **96**

in art **83**, **91**, 94, **97**

in literature 94–6

mirrors 18

Monymusk reliquary 115

mother goddesses 42, **46**, 135

in triads 42, 60, 63, **63**

moustaches **7**, 110, **121**, **128**

music **104**, 107, **107**

mythology **8**, **33**, **44**, **50**, 94–9, 108, 135

see also religion

N

Navan Fort, County Armagh 32

Neara Mac Niadhain, Irish mythical hero 99

neck-rings *see* torcs

nemeton (sacred grove) 32

nymphs **34**

O

Oengus, Irish mythical hero 94–5

oral traditions 25

Otherworld

entrances to **38**, 66, **70**

islands of **67**

journeys to 66–9, **66**, **67**, 135

permeable boundary with reality 66, 93, 94, 98, 99, **100**

P

Paps of Anu **48**

Parisi, Gaulish tribe 50, **52**

Patrick, St.

bell shrine **117**

brought Christianity to Ireland **76**

hand bell 115

phalerae (horse harnesses) **19**, **21**, **63**, **132**

Picts (*Picti*; "Painted Ones") 110

plant motifs 18, **59**, 74, **83**

Pliny the Elder (23–79CE), Roman historian **59**

Po Valley **93**

Poulnabrone megalithic tomb **70**

R

religion

cycle of death and rebirth 96

decapitation, role of **102**, 125

funeral rites 102–103

monasticism 74, **76**, 86–7, **87**

nature deities **9**, **24**, 28

oral transmission of 104

pantheon of gods 28

places of worship 27, 32

rituals 32, **59**

Roman tolerance of **103**

sacrifices 37, 102, **102**, 104, 125

votive offerings 32, **34**, 35, 37, **53**, **108**, **131**

warrior cult **102**, 121, 125, **125**

water, spiritual power of 34–7, **34**, **35**, **37**

see also bards; druids

reliquaries **107**, 114–15, **115**, 117

Remi, Gaulish tribe 60

Rhiannon, Otherworld woman **64**, 98, 135

ringfort, Grianan Aileach 130, **133**

rivers 34, **37**

Rome, sacked by Celts 13

Roquepertuse, Saluvii sanctuary **20**, 125, **125**

S

St. Maur en Chausée, Celtic
sanctuary **125**
saints 106–7
see also evangelists, four;
individual saints' names
salt deposits, Hallstatt **7**, 10
Saluvi, Gaulish tribe **20**, **102**, 125
Samhain ("End of Summer")
festival 66, 98, **98**, 99
sandstone figure **132**
scabbard **34**
script *see* letter decoration
sculpture
on axe–heads **19**
bronze **7**
on cauldrons **8**, 24
stone carvings **20**, 21, **32**, **37**, 52,
118, 122
shields 13, 37, **122**
for display and ceremonial
130–31
sidhe (pre-Celtic barrows) *see* burial
mounds
silver-gilt 14, **27**
snake symbolism 49, 50, **50**, 95
Snowdonia, Wales **38**
spiral patterns **23**
stags **28**, 50, **50**, 52, **52**, **97**

T

Taliesin, Welsh poet-hero **33**, 94,
98
"Tara Brooch" **14**
Taranis **31**
tattoos 110
Telamon 13
Thames river **130**, **131**
torcs 9, **10**, 24, **28**, **50**, 52, **52**,
110, **110**

Strabo (ca. 64BCE–ca. 21CE),
Greek writer 8, 32, 35, 104,
106, 122, 125
Strettweg chariot 52
sun disks **112**
decorated **34**
swords **122**, 130
symbolism
animals **90**
bulls 60–63
eternal knot **79**
horses 134
in jewelry **112**
La Tène style 21
ram-headed snake 49, 50, **50**
religious **90**
Tree of Life **55**

ceremonial or religious use **110**
decoration **110**, **113**
on statues **27**, **95**
status symbols **10**, 52, 113
worn by deities 9, **42**, **95**, 113
worn by warriors 113, 122, **128**,
132
trade 10
salt **7**, 10–12
Tree of Life, symbolism of **55**
trees, decorative **12**
Treveri tribe 31, 42
triplication 28, 60–63
genii cucullati 63, **63**
goddesses 42, 45, 60, **60**, 63, **63**
heads 60, **63**, 125
in literature 63
triskele motif **60**, 63
Tuatha Dé Danann, inhabitants of
Otherworld 46, 66–7, **70**, 99
see also goddess, Danu

V

victory ceremonies **102**, 103
Vikings 74, 80, 114, 117
vines **55**
Virgin, mother of Christ 84, **84**,
89

Vix, Burgundy, jewelry from grave
110, 113

W

Wales
law **104**, 106, **121**
Mabinogi tales **38**, 63, **64**, 69, 96,
98, 135
mythology 96, 98–9
war trumpets (*carnyces*) 132
warriors
appearance 14, **121**, **128**, **132**
cavalry 134, **134**, 135
society 8, 13, 121, 122–5
see also armor; arms
watchtowers **117**
weapons *see* armor; arms
wells and springs 34, **34**, 35, 108
Madron Well **108**
White Island, Co. Fermanagh
86–7, **87**
willow tree **55**, **107**
women
grave goods **110**
in manuscript decoration 84, **84**
in priestly roles 45
status 42, 45

PICTURE CREDITS

The publisher should like to thank the following people, museums, and photographic libraries for permission to reproduce their material. Every care has been taken to trace copyright holders. However, if we have omitted anyone we apologize and will, if informed, make corrections in any future edition.

Abbreviations
t top; **c** center; **b** bottom; **l** left; **r** right
BAL: Bridgeman
MSP: Mick Sharp Photography
NMC: National Museum of Copenhagen
NMI: National Museum of Ireland
WFA: Werner Foreman Archive

Cover Jean Williamson/MSP; **page 1** BM; **2** Paul Wakefield/Getty Images; **3** Dagli Orti; **6** The Stock Market; **7** AKG, London; **8** NMC; **9** Dagli Orti; **10** Piero Baguzzi/Gruppo Editoriale Fabbri, Italy; **12** AKG, London; **13** BM; **14l** BM/BAL; **14r** BM/WFA; **15** Staatliche Museen zu Berlin/BAL; **16–17** MSP; **18** AKG, London; **19** DBP Archive; **20** Dagli Orti; **21** BM/AKG, London; **22** Trinity College Library, Dublin; **23** Piero Baguzzi/Gruppo Editoriale Fabbri, Italy; **24** NMC; **25** Dagli Orti; **26** Paul Wakefield/Getty Images; **27** AKG, London; **28** AKG, London; **29** Dagli Orti; **30** Dagli Orti; **30 background** Ralph Wetmore/Getty Images; **31** AKG, London; **32** MSP; **33** Paul Wakefield/Getty Images; **34t** Museum of Antiquities/CM Dixon; **34b** AKG, London; **35** Fortean Picture Library; **36** The Stock Market; **37** The Roman Baths Museum, Bath; **38–39** Jean Williamson/MSP; **40** NMC/AKG, London; **42** National Library of Wales; **43** NMC/AKG, London; **44** National Library of Wales; **45l** e.t. Archive; **45r** Dagli Orti; **46–7** The Slide File; **48** NMC; **49** NMC; **50** National Library of Wales; **51** NMC/AKG, London; **52** CM Dixon; **53** The Stock Market; **54** Trinity College Library, Dublin; **56–7** Connie Coleman/Getty Images; **59** Piero Baguzzi/Gruppo Editoriale Fabbri, Italy; **60** Ulster Museum; **61** CM Dixon/Housesteads Museum; **62** Museo Civico Romano, Brescia/e.t. Archive; **63** CM Dixon/Housesteads Museum; **64** University of Cambridge/DBP; **66** NMI/WFA; **67** MSP; **68** BM/AKG, London; **69** Naturhistorisches Museum, Vienna/AKG, London; **70–71** Paul Harris/Getty Images; **72** Trinity College Library, Dublin; **74** National Library of Wales; **75** BL/e.t. Archive; **76** MSP; **77** Fitzwilliam Museum, University of Cambridge; **80** Trinity College Library, Dublin; **81** MSP; **82** British Library; **83** Royal Irish Academy, Dublin; **84** BL/BAL; **85** Trinity College Library, Dublin; **86** BAL/Lichfield Cathedral; **87** Images Colour Library; **89** The Library, St John's College, University of Cambridge (Ms.C.5 f.35r); **90** BL/BAL; **92** Images Colour Library; **93** BM/AKG, London; **94** BM/WFA; **95** Dagli Orti; **96** Moravska Museum, Czech Republic/AKG, London; **97** National Library of Wales; **98** WFA/Musée de Rennes; **99** Musee de la Civilisation Gallo-Romano, Consiel General du Rhone; **100–101** Alain le Garsmeur/Image Ireland; **102** Musee Granet/AKG, London; **103** Scope; **104l** Dagli Orti; **104r** BM/DBP; **105** National Library of Wales; **106** MSP; **107** NMI; **108** MSP; **109** The Roman Baths Museum, Bath; **110** Naturhistorisches Museum, Vienna/AKG, London; **111** Dagli Orti; **112** Naturhistorisches Museum, Vienna/AKG, London; **113t** Piero Baguzzi/Gruppo Editoriale Fabbri, Italy; **113b** Kelten Museum, Hallein, Austria/AKG, London; **114** The Slide File; **115** NMI/AKG, London; **116** NMI; **117** The Slide File; **118** The Slide File; **120** NMC; **121** National Library of Wales; **122** National Library of Wales; **123** Naturhistorisches Museum, Vienna/AKG, London; **124** National Museum, Ljubljana/AKG, London; **125** Piero Baguzzi/Gruppo Editoriale Fabbri, Italy; **126–7** The Slide File; **128** National Museum of Prague/AKG, London; **129** NMC; **130l** e.t. Archive; **130** BM/AKG, London; **131** BM/AKG, London; **132l** DBP Archives; **132r** Wuerttemburgisches Museum/AKG, London; **133** Alain le Garsmeur/Image Ireland; **134** NMC; **135** BM/AKG, London; **136** BM/Michael Holford

Further caption information
page 22 Carpet page from the medieval Book of Durrow.
page 23 Silver phalera from the treasure hoard of Chao de Lamas, Spain.
page 40 Figure riding a dolphin, from the Gundestrup Cauldron.
page 48 Animal figure from the Gundestrup Cauldron.
page 49 Winged creature from the Gundestrup Cauldron.
page 54 Geneaology of Christ from the Lindisfarne Gospels (ca. 700CE).
page 59 The "Agris helmet" from Charente, France (4th century BCE; gold-plated iron, decorated with bronze, silver, and coral).
page 83 Letter "M" opens this page from the Cathach of St. Columba psalter (ca. 600CE).
page 89 Crucifixion of Christ from the Southampton Psalter.
page 90 Winged ox of St. Luke from the Lindisfarne Gospels (ca. 700CE).
page 118 10th-century stone cross from Monasterboice, Co. Louth, Ireland.
page 128 3rd-century-BCE male head wearing a torc, from Zehrovice in Bohemia.
page 129 Male warrior head from a silver disk (ca. 1st century BCE; Manerbio, Italy).